RELIGIOUS AND
ANTI-RELIGIOUS THOUGHT
IN RUSSIA

F L
W

FRANK L. WEIL

INSTITUTE FOR

STUDIES IN

RELIGION AND

THE HUMANITIES

RELIGIOUS

AND

ANTI-RELIGIOUS

THOUGHT IN

RUSSIA

GEORGE L. KLINE

The Weil Lectures

CHICAGO & LONDON

THE UNIVERSITY OF CHICAGO PRESS

Library of Congress Catalog Card Number: 68-54484

THE UNIVERSITY OF CHICAGO PRESS, CHICAGO 60637
The University of Chicago Press, Ltd., London W.C. 1

To the Memory of

LILLIAN C. HARDY

FOREWORD

Unlike some of my predecessors in the series of Weil lecturers who have delivered directly publishable lectures, I have found that my lectures needed to be reworked and expanded. I have also supplied the scholarly references that seemed essential in a study—based in large part on untranslated Russian sources—that involves the exploration of one or two relatively unblazed intellectual trails. I apologize for the profusion of footnotes and hope that they will not deter readers who might otherwise be interested in my topic.

My sincere thanks to Dr. William C. Fletcher for his helpful suggestions and critical comments on an earlier version of chapter 6 and to Dr. Andrew Q. Blane for his astute and constructive criticisms of the Introduction and of portions of chapters 4, 5, and 6.

The titles of Russian books and journals are given in the widely used Library of Congress transliteration system, slightly simplified.

I am deeply appreciative of the honor implied by the invitation to join the distinguished company of Weil lecturers. It is a special pleasure to recall the warmth of my Cincinnati welcome in the hospitable homes of Dr. and Mrs. Samuel Sandmel, Dr. and Mrs. Nelson Glueck, and my old friends Dr. and Mrs. Van Meter Ames.

GEORGE L. KLINE

Bryn Mawr College

CONTENTS

INTRODUCTION

This study is focused upon religious *thought*—both philosophy of religion, broadly conceived, and philosophical theology (theistic and non-theistic)—and upon anti-religious thought—what might be called "philosophical atheology." In treating the Soviet period (chapter 6) I shall also have something to say about religious *institutions*; and in dealing with such critics as Bakunin, Tolstoy, Leontyev, and Rozanov (chapters 1 and 2) I shall consider some of the religious institutions and practices which they criticized.

This study covers only the last one hundred years: Bakunin and Leontyev began writing on religious topics in the mid-1860's, and Tolstoy's *Confession* was written in 1879. The century between the mid-1860's and the mid-1960's has been exceptionally fruitful for Russian religious thought and exceptionally fateful for Russian religious practice, especially the Soviet period. Still, one might have pressed back to the early nineteenth century: to the Slavophiles in the 1840's and 1850's, to Chaadayev in the 1830's, even to Skovoroda in the late eighteenth century. I have not included the Slavophiles (Khomyakov, the Kireyevskis, Aksakov, and Samarin) or Chaadayev, because they are relatively well known—better known than, say, Leontyev, Rozanov, or Shestov. I have not included Skovoroda for a quite different reason: this "Russian Socrates," a Christian mystic and neo-Stoic, is very little known and deserves to be treated, both as philosopher and religious thinker, in a separate study.

All of the ten thinkers who receive separate treatment here are "exemplary" thinkers who represent pure and extreme positions in the history of religious and anti-religious thought in Russia. All of them, as it happened, made their intellectual mark before 1917. This applies not only to Plekhanov (who died in 1918) and Rozanov (d. 1919) but also to Lenin (d. 1924), Lunacharski (d. 1933), and Gorky (d. 1936). The relevant writings of the three last-named date from the decade before the First World War.

The ten thinkers whom I shall discuss differ sharply. First, they differ in their attitude toward religion, which ranges from that of Shestov, a quite orthodox though "existentialist" and "irrationalist" Jew, and Berdyaev, a near-heretical but "Orthodox" existentialist, through that of Tolstoy, Leontyev, and Rozanov—all of whom rejected essential aspects of nineteenth-century Christianity—through that of Gorky and Lunacharski, the secular and socialist "God-builders," to that of Plekhanov and Lenin, who rejected religion of every kind, including the Prometheanism of their fellow Marxist "God-builders."

They also differ in intellectual power and profundity. Bakunin, Gorky, Lunacharski, Plekhanov, Lenin, and even Tolstoy lack the originality and depth of thought that mark Leontyev, Rozanov, Shestov, and—with some qualifications—Berdyaev.

The three among these thinkers who were most original—Leontyev, Rozanov, and Shestov—seem to me more provocative and profound than their contemporaries, such as Vladimir Solovyov (who was superior to all of them as a speculative system-builder but inferior, in my judgment, as a philosopher of religion and philosophical theologian), S. L. Frank, and Fathers

2

Paul Florensky and Serge Bulgakov. Still, Solovyov is not wholly neglected in this study because his influence makes itself felt in the thought of Berdyaev and, to a lesser extent, Rozanov.

Dostoyevski is a special case. I have not devoted a separate chapter or half-chapter to his religious thought; however, since he powerfully influenced Rozanov, Berdyaev, and Shestov, and drew sharp criticism from Leontyev, his name will figure prominently in these pages.[1]

In addition to the unity and continuity afforded by the shared critical or constructive concern with religion on the part of all ten thinkers, there are two further, less substantial kinds of continuity. First, there is the circumstance that several of these thinkers commented on each other's work. Berdyaev wrote detailed commentaries on Tolstoy, Leontyev, and Shestov, as well as acute criticisms of Marxism—in the form given the doctrine by Marx himself and also in its reformulations by Plekhanov and Lenin. Leontyev criticized Tolstoy's position. Rozanov discussed Tolstoy, Leontyev, and Berdyaev. Shestov commented at length on Tolstoy and Berdyaev, and briefly on Rozanov.

Second, a thread (a "red thread," as Marxists like to say) of violent anti-religion extends from Bakunin through Lenin to the Soviet period, and finds partial echoes in some of the more polemical views of Tolstoy, Leontyev, and—in a special way—Rozanov.

All of these thinkers, but the Marxists somewhat less clearly than the non-Marxists, exhibit four features that have been widely exemplified in Russian religious (and philosophical) thought.

[1] For a sympathetic and perceptive discussion of Dostoyevski's religious views, see V. V. Zenkovsky, *A History of Russian Philosophy*, trans. George L. Kline (London: Routledge & Kegan Paul; New York: Columbia University Press, 1953). 1: 410–32; reprinted in René Wellek, ed., *Dostoevsky: A Collection of Critical Essays* (Englewood Cliffs, N.J.: Prentice-Hall, 1963), pp. 130–45.

3

1. Russian speculation has generally centered on man. Sometimes, as among the Marxists, it has centered on man as a biological species or as a historical collectivity; but more often—as in Leontyev, Rozanov, Shestov, and Berdyaev—it centered on men as existing individuals: *lichnosti*.[2] From the beginnings of religious speculation in the sixteenth century and of philosophical speculation in the eighteenth century, attention has centered on such themes as the meaning of individual existence; the problem of moral choice, freedom, and responsibility; the pattern and purpose of history; and the relation of religion to general culture.

Russian thinkers turned late, and hesitantly, to such technical disciplines as epistemology (they were more interested in what we know than in how we know it) and cosmology (they were more interested in man than in the world). Russia's philosophical theology and systematic metaphysics, as well as its philosophy of religion, have had a uniquely close connection with philosophical anthropology, ethics, social philosophy, and the philosophy of history.

2. Related to the focus on the individual person has been a special "existential" intensity and an impatience with moderation. Rusian thinkers have typically been theists or anti-theists, not agnostics. This is one reason why Nietzsche has had such a

[2] The Russian word *lichnost* (plural *lichnosti*) can mean "individual," "person," or "individual person," and is sometimes translated "personality." The man-centeredness of Russian religious and philosophical thought is epitomized by the titles of two of the earliest and two of the most recent works by Russian thinkers: Gregory Skovoroda's *Narcissus: A Dialogue on the Theme "Know Thyself"* (written ca. 1766) and Alexander Radishchev's treatise *On Man, His Mortality and Immortality* (1796), and the posthumous works of two of the major Russian religious thinkers of the twentieth century, Berdyaev's *Self-Knowledge: An Essay in Philosophical Autobiography* (1949) (translated into English as *Dream and Reality*) and S. L. Frank's *Reality and Man* (1956).

powerful appeal in Russia. We recall Dostoyevski's passionate young men, arguing until dawn about God and immortality; the dramatic confrontation of Ivan and Alyosha Karamazov; and Ivan's "Legend of the Grand Inquisitor."

One such "Dostoyevskian" discussion had raged for several hours (in the 1830's) among a group that included Turgenev, then a rising young writer, and the critic Belinski. It was growing late, and Turgenev, exhausted by the interminable talk, suggested that the group adjourn for supper. Belinski's impassioned and scornful rejoinder has become classic: "We have not yet settled the question of whether God exists, and you want to eat!"

3. In Russia, more than elsewhere, the major literary figures have been deeply concerned with religious questions. One thinks of such prose writers as Gogol, Tolstoy, Dostoyevski, and Pasternak, and of such poets as Fet, Blok, Tsvetayeva, Pasternak, and, among the younger Soviet generation, Brodsky. A number of religious thinkers, moreover, have been gifted, if minor, poets: Skovoroda, Khomyakov, Vladimir Solovyov.

4. Related both to its intensity and its involvement with *belles lettres* is the fact that Russian religious thought has been uniquely non-academic and non-institutional. One could scarcely discuss American or European religious philosophy of the late nineteenth and twentieth century without reference to such university professors as Otto, Royce, William James, Whitehead, Barth, Buber, Bergson, Maritain, Marcel, Niebuhr, and Tillich, but in Russia the original and influential religious thinkers (originality of thought has not always coincided with influence, as we shall see—especially in the case of Leontyev and Rozanov) have almost without exception been non-academic. Professors of philosophy and theology in the Russian universities and theological academies have tended to follow one or another Western, Russian, or Byzantine master rather than

5

strike out on their own to plow fresh intellectual furrows. Solovyov and Rozanov are exceptions, but both of them left the academic world while they were still in their thirties.

It is significant that none of the ten Russian thinkers whom I shall discuss in detail was a university professor; all, except Lenin and perhaps Tolstoy and Gorky, were in a broad sense "critics." Their West European counterparts would be such thinkers as Kierkegaard, John Stuart Mill, Nietzsche (who, like Solovyov and Rozanov, *began* as an academic), Matthew Arnold, and Camus. Most of these Russians made their living by writing (book reviews, articles, books); professionally, most of them were *hommes de lettres*. But "letters" in Russia (the Russian word is *literatura*) has always been conceived generously enough to include social, political, and philosophical commentary as well as poetry, drama, the novel, and the short story. Most of these Russians were political, social, and cultural critics—not merely, or even primarily, literary critics. And much of their criticism of politics, society, and culture was focused upon religion and the church.

The Western thinker who most pervasively influenced this galaxy was Nietzsche, in ways too complicated to summarize here. The impact of Nietzsche's thought was clearest in the religious existentialists Shestov and Berdyaev, and the Marxist "God-builders" Gorky and Lunacharski. But Leontyev and Rozanov were "Russian Nietzscheans"—as Alexander Herzen to a degree had been—*avant la lettre*.

Two minor characteristics of the ten thinkers also may be worth brief mention.

1. Seven of them—Bakunin, Plekhanov, Lenin, Lunacharski, Gorky, Shestov, and Berdyaev—spent most or all of their mature years in Western Europe. All of them, however—except Bakunin, who wrote mostly in French—continued to write and

publish in their native Russian. The other three men—Tolstoy, Leontyev, and Rozanov—lived out their lives in Russia, rarely even visiting Western Europe (Leontyev spent ten years in Greece and Turkey).

2. Rozanov shocked his contemporaries by equating atheism with asexuality and asserting a close connection between religion and sex. I shall mention the sexual peculiarities of three of the ten thinkers only in order to set aside, as inappropriate for exploration here, the possible effect of such peculiarities upon their religious views. Apart from the inadequacy of Freudian and neo-Freudian reductionist "interpretations" of theoretical positions, there is the plain and relevant fact that Rozanov and Shestov, who were sexually quite normal, expressed religious philosophies as immoderate as those of any of their less normal compatriots.[3]

Next a word about some general characteristics of Russian Orthodoxy. If we distinguish between intellectual, social, and strictly religious or spiritual aspects of religion, we shall find that the Russian Orthodox tradition has always emphasized the last of these to the virtual exclusion of the first two. It has had few creative theologians and has been almost entirely innocent of social or civic involvement. Social work and social service, even discussion of public issues, has generally been foreign to the Russian religious mind. Philanthropy and charity have been unorganized, purely individual matters, even when religiously motivated. Critics of Russian Orthodoxy have complained at least since the mid-nineteenth century that the Russian church is extremely weak in the sphere of public or social life, precisely where the Western churches were strong.[4]

---

[3] Bakunin was impotent; Leontyev was said to be bisexual (homosexual as well as heterosexual); and reports persist that Berdyaev's long-term marriage was never consummated. Of course, Tolstoy in his later years preached, but managed only imperfectly to practice, sexual abstinence.

[4] Thus Alexander Koshelyov wrote to Alexis Khomyakov (December 1,

In chapter 6 I shall indicate how this historically rooted de-emphasis of social concern has been exploited by the Soviet authorities in their attack upon religion. Initially, however, I want to mark off this lack of social concern from a related but distinct phenomenon: the political involvement and privilege of the church hierarchy. Political involvement at the top is quite compatible with social non-involvement at the bottom, and even at the middle, of the body ecclesiastic. In Russia responsibility for social action and social service, including organized philanthropy, has always been assumed to rest with "the authorities," no clear distinction having been drawn in this regard between secular and ecclesiastical authorities.

In Tsarist Russia, of course, there was no sharp separation of church and state; the Russian Orthodox church, at least from Peter the Great onward, was a kind of state church. Curiously, it has again become a (perhaps negative) kind of state church, in the sense of being least disadvantaged of any of the religious organizations that are now permitted to function in the Soviet Union.

A glance ahead may serve as orientation in what for some readers will be a strange intellectual landscape.

The first chapter deals with two aspects of one of the earliest

---

1853) that the Roman Catholic chuch is permeated with and illuminated by the "practical, visible aspect of life," that it strives to "bring Christianity into private and especially social life." The Russian Orthodox church, he continued, is not "of this world" in the sense that Catholicism is: "Our Church can and should borrow from the Western church its knowledge of, and influence upon, this world—in a word, its efficacy." (In N. P. Kolyupanov, *Biografiya Aleksandra Ivanovicha Koshelyova* [A Biography of Alexander Ivanovich Koshelyov] [Moscow, 1892], vol. 2, app. 14, p. 77.) Even earlier Peter Chaadayev had written to the French Count Sircour (1845): "Our church is essentially ascetic, just as yours is essentially social. . . ." (*Sochineniya i pisma P. Ya. Chaadayeva* [The Works and Letters of P. Ya. Chaadayev], ed. M. O. Gershenzon, 2 vols. [Moscow, 1913–1914], 1:254).

sustained critiques to be leveled at organized religion by Russian thinkers—that of the anarchists. Bakunin, who was primarily a *political* anarchist, rejected religion of every kind, not just its institutionalized historical forms. Tolstoy, who was mainly a *cultural* anarchist, rejected every kind of institutionalized religion but offered his own one-sided reading of New Testament ethics as the "true Christianity."

The second chapter deals with two Russian critics who were radically dissatisfied with nineteenth-century Christianity. Leontyev saw its dominant thrust as facilitating the secular slide toward universal mediocrity, egalitarianism, and socialism. Rozanov rejected New Testament asceticism in favor of a life-affirming "metaphysics of sex and family life," for which he found support in the Old Testament.

The third chapter deals with two religious existentialists, the "irrationalist" Shestov and the "personalist" Berdyaev. Both men rejected systematic theology, as well as various aspects of institutionalized religion, as incompatible with the freedom of the "existing individual."

The fourth chapter considers the "God-builders," Gorky and Lunacharski, who attempted between, say, 1905 and 1914 to found a new Promethean "religion of socialism" or "religion of mankind." Lenin, as we shall see, brutally repudiated their attempt as a backsliding into fideism.

The fifth chapter is devoted to the Marxist critique of religion: Plekhanov's intellectualist view of religion as innocent superstition and Lenin's practicalist view of religion as an arm of bourgeois politics.

Relatively individualistic thought on religious questions did not last beyond the 1920's in the Soviet Union. Gorky and Lunacharski, who lived on into the 1930's, renounced their pre-revolutionary religion of "God-building" and joined the snowballing movement of Leninist anti-religious militance. Accordingly, the sixth and final chapter deals not with individual thinkers but with the survival of religion and the career of official anti-religion in the Soviet half-century between 1917 and 1967.

I distinguish two pseudo-religious surrogates and one genuinely religious surrogate for traditional religions in the Soviet Union today: (1) orthodoxly atheistic Marxism-Leninism;[5] (2) a scientific-technological Prometheanism, unacknowledged heir to the earlier pseudo-religion of "God-building"; and (3) something relatively new—a "philosophical" and mostly non-ecclesiastical theism that often borders on pantheism.

Among adherents of this third kind on non-traditional religion, as well as among the few Soviet intellectuals whose religious commitment takes traditional forms, interest in the thought of Rozanov, Shestov, and Berdyaev is surprisingly strong and is growing stronger. The quiet rediscovery of these long proscribed thinkers is one of the most exciting features of the current intellectual scene in the Soviet Union.

[5] Cf. Dostoyevski's penetrating remark that only in Russia could atheism become a kind of religion.

10

1

THE ANARCHIST CRITIQUE: BAKUNIN AND TOLSTOY

It is not usual to link Bakunin and Tolstoy as thinkers. Bakunin, who was born in 1814, died in 1876—too early to witness the "spiritual crisis" that led Tolstoy to his obsessive concern with ethical and religious questions. Yet Bakunin's anarchism, like that of his fellow countryman, Prince Peter Kropotkin, found a clear echo in Tolstoy's later position.

There has probably never been a theoretically consistent anarchist; in any case, Bakunin and Tolstoy had their share of inconsistencies. Bakunin in his last years sought to realize his socio-political ideal of absolute individual freedom by means of a dictatorial revolutionary party that subjected individual revolutionaries to its centralizing authority. Tolstoy in his later years— from about 1880 onward—sought to realize the ethics of absolute non-violence through the application of what might be called "intellectual coercion." He was quite prepared to browbeat non-Tolstoyans into acceptance of a Tolstoyan position!

Both Bakunin and Tolstoy, from their early years, were self-assured and intellectually arrogant Russian noblemen, impatient with anyone who failed to embrace their obvious and total "truth." There was a strong strain of political violence in Baku-

11

nin's anarchism, and more than a hint of personal authoritarianism in Tolstoy's rejection of traditional authorities.

I

Michael Alexandrovich Bakunin was born, in the words of his friend Alexander Herzen, "not under a fixed star but under a comet." For our purposes the relevant facts about Bakunin's stormy life are his youthful rebellion against parental and military authority, his early absorption in German idealist philosophy, and his subsequent turn (in Western Europe) to revolutionary action. Herzen also remarked, unflatteringly but not unjustly, that Bakunin "served for a year or two in the artillery and a year or two in Moscow Hegelianism."[1] Imprisoned for his part in the revolutions of 1848 and 1849 in France and Germany, Bakunin remained in Siberian exile until 1861, when he escaped from Russia and made his way to England via Japan and the United States. He was to spend the rest of his life in Western Europe, dying in Bern in 1876.

Bakunin was neither an original nor a consistent, let alone systematic, thinker. The anarcho-socialism for which he is best known is to be found substantially complete in Proudhon and Stirner. His other themes were drawn ready made from the intellectual warehouses of the eighteenth and nineteenth centuries. He shared Rousseau's faith in the "radical goodness" of human nature—uncorrupted by evil (mainly religious and political) institutions—and Comte's anti-metaphysical fervor. He accepted the basic tenets of Marx's economic determinism, Darwin's emphasis upon the struggle for existence, Hegel's dialectic—in a Proudhonian version that reduced the triad to

[1] A. I. Herzen, *Byloye i dumy*, pt. 5, in *Sobraniye sochineni* [Collected Works] (Moscow, 1956), 10:316; English translation, *My Past and Thoughts: The Memoirs of Alexander Herzen*, trans. Constance Garnett (London, 1924), 3:256.

a dyad, stressing opposition rather than reconciliation—and Hegel's insight into the massive influence of the social and cultural milieu. After 1861 he embraced the reigning atheism and materialism of the time. He echoed Feuerbach's "anthropological" account of religion and drew his critique of contemporary political, economic, and social institutions largely from Saint-Simon, Fourier, Proudhon, and Marx. Bakunin added passion, intemperance, and a charge of nihilism—formulated with polemical sparkle and rhetorical persuasiveness. According to those who knew him, he had great personal magnetism.

It was not until the mid-1860's, at the age of fifty, that Bakunin for the first time became a convinced and fervent atheist. He had been anti-clerical and anti-ecclesiastical in temper before this, but not atheistic. In fact, as a young man he had been sentimentally devout and inclined toward mysticism; he reasserted his belief in personal immortality as late as 1843, when he was twenty-nine. In 1849, at age thirty-five, he declared that he no longer sought to comprehend God through Hegelian philosophy but now sought God in "human freedom" and in "revolution."[2]

What was it that led Bakunin, in middle age, to atheism and materialism? It seems clear that his motives were not philosophical, nor even intellectual; rather, he was moved by a powerful need to defend and justify his own pre-philosophical values. He had long been committed to the moral-social values of absolute freedom and equality; he now came to regard this commitment as incompatible with religious belief of any kind.

In such a use of materialism and atheism, of course, Bakunin is not alone. The major materialists and atheists, beginning with

[2] A convenient compilation of Bakunin's anti-religious views is to be found in The Political Philosophy of Bakunin: Scientific Anarchism, ed. G. P. Maximoff (Glencoe, Ill.: Free Press, 1953), pt. 1, chs. 10–11, pp. 105–20.

13

Epicurus and Lucretius and extending through Hobbes, Holbach, Lamettrie, Helvetius, and Diderot to Marx and Lenin, have used their philosophical materialism to support their atheism, which in turn was used to defend moral, social, and political values and aims whose genesis and motivation lay elsewhere.

Epicurus and Lucretius used their reductive materialistic atomism as a weapon to combat the paralyzing fear of a painful afterlife and the caprices of cruel deities. Lucretius was especially incensed at the inhumanities men perpetrate upon each other in the name of religion. The example to which the poet constantly recurs is Agamemnon's sacrifice of his innocent daughter, Iphigenia, to appease the offended Artemis and persuade the goddess to release the sea winds so that the Greeks could sail for Troy. Since the soul also—Lucretius argues—is made up of atoms that are dispersed at the death of the body, death is utter oblivion and nothingness: "Where I am death is not, and where death is I am not."

Philosophically speaking, Lucretius' atomism—like that of Democritus and Epicurus, upon which it was based—was not very adequate, even in his own day. Its materialistic interpretations of such phenomena as sense perception and memory are often far-fetched, sometimes self-contradictory. Lucretius, one assumes, must have been aware of at least some of the difficulties of his position, but he clung to his materialism as a thoretical support for his anti-religion.

The French anti-clerics of the eighteenth century followed the same tack. Accept materialism, they preached to le peuple, discard your superstitious beliefs in God, the soul, the afterlife, and you will be liberated for revolutionary action in this world. Your present sufferings will not be rewarded in another world. To believe otherwise is to be duped and dulled—as Marx was later to say—by the "opium" of religion.

14

Although the socio-political aims of the *philosophes* were more clearly defined, their theoretical materialism showed no significant advance over that of the ancient atomists. Yet the intervening centuries had seen much searching criticism of philosophical materialism—by thinkers of the first rank, including Descartes, Leibniz, Berkeley, and Kant. Neither the French materialists nor (what is more to our purpose) Bakunin made any serious attempt to answer these criticisms, or to refine and strengthen materialism as a philosophical position. Indeed, Bakunin defined his prime category, "matter," so broadly as to include virtually anything imaginable—except, of course, anything that could be construed as a support for religious beliefs or practices.

"By these words 'matter' and 'material,'" he declared, "we mean the totality, the whole spectrum of real entities (*êtres*), known and unknown, from the simplest organic bodies to the structure and functioning of the brain of the greatest genius: the finest (*les plus beaux*) *feelings*, the greatest *thoughts*, heroic acts . . . as well as . . . electricity, light, heat, . . ."[3] Materialism, for Bakunin, is the philosophy that accepts "matter" in this diffuse and inflated sense as the sole reality. Its opposite, idealism, is the philosophy that asserts the reality of something "nonmaterial" or spiritual. Logically speaking, Bakunin's argument against "idealism" is circular; in effect, he offers us the following "proof."

Why must we accept philosophical materialism? *Because the only alternative is philosophical idealism, and idealism leads to religion.*

But why must we reject religion? *Because religion makes false claims, asserting the existence of non-material entities.*

[3] Mikhail Bakunin, "Réponse d'un International à Mazzini," in *Oeuvres* (Paris, 1913), 6:117 (italics added).

But why should we refuse to admit non-material entities? *Because we accept materialism.*

But why must we accept materialism? *Da capo al fine!*

In a word, Bakunin's atheism rests upon his materialism and his materialism, in turn, rests upon his atheism. This did not bother Bakunin (nor Lenin, who later adopted essentially the same position) because his reasons for accepting both atheism and materialism lay elsewhere.

Bakunin admitted the universality of religious belief, but concluded from this fact only that the idea of God is a "necessary [i.e., historically inevitable] error" in man's development. It was "the action of man's brain" that created the gods. "All the religions with their gods were never anything else but the creation of the believing and credulous fantasy of men. . . ."[4]

Bakunin's explanation of how men came to misdirect their reverence and piety, worshiping God instead of mankind, adds nothing to Feuerbach's account except rhetorical violence. "Heaven, the dwelling-place of the immortal gods," Bakunin declared, "is nothing but a distorting mirror which sends back to the believer his own image in an inverted and swollen form."[5]

Bakunin's only non-circular argument for atheism is an ethical one. Theism, he maintained, is incompatible with the reality of human freedom. The existence of God is "the negation of human freedom. . . . Anyone who wants to worship God must renounce his freedom and human dignity."[6]

---

[4] "Fédéralisme, socialisme, et antithéologisme," in Oeuvres, 1:61.

[5] *Ibid.*, pp. 131 f. Feuerbach's own rhetoric, we may note, was sometimes fairly violent, as when he called contemporary Christians "religious and political lackeys of a monarchy both heavenly and earthly" (*Vorlesungen über das Wesen der Religion* [1851], in Ludwig Feuerbach, *Sämtliche Werke* (Stuttgart, 1903–11 [reprinted in 1960]), 8:29).

[6] "Fédéralisme," in Oeuvres, 1:64. The editors of Bakunin's posthumous writings have utilized similar, and even identical, texts in more than one work. For example, the passage just quoted from "Fédéralisme" also appears

Bakunin summed up his argument in a celebrated syllogism, which logicians will recognize as a formally valid mixed hypothetical inference in the *modus tollendo tollens*—"denying the consequent." Masaryk has called it an "ontological proof of atheism,"[7] a label that is clever but inexact. It might better be called an "ethical" or "anthropological" proof. It runs as follows.

"If God exists, then man is a slave; but man is . . . free [i.e., man is not a slave]; therefore, God does not exist." Of course, the central question concerns not the formal validity of the syllogism but the truth of its major premise: "If God exists, man is a slave." This appears self-evident to Bakunin, and he plays endless variations on the theme. For example: "God being everything, the real world and man are nothing"; "God being master, man is the slave."[8]

Bakunin does not shrink even from the hyper-Promethean conclusion that follows from his position. "If God [actually] existed," he wrote in 1871, "he could serve human freedom in only one way—by ceasing to exist. . . . I reverse Voltaire's aphorism and say: 'If God really existed, it would be necessary to abolish him.' "[9] Nothing could indicate more clearly the moral and political basis of Bakunin's theomachy. His rejection of God is not the outcome of theoretical doubt or philosophical inquiry but of a practical and moral need.

Bakunin summed up his indictment by contrasting what he

in *God and the State*, preface by Carlo Cafiero and Elisée Reclus (New York, 1916[?]), p. 25.

[7] Thomas G. Masaryk, *The Spirit of Russia*, trans. Eden and Cedar Paul (London and New York: Macmillan, 1955), 1:447.

[8] "Fédéralisme" in Oeuvres, 1:64, 63; also in *God and the State* p. 25. Cf. Feuerbach: "To enrich God, man must become poor; that God may be all, man must be nothing" (*Das Wesen des Christentums* [1841], *Sämtliche Werke*, 6:32; also *The Essence of Christianity*, trans. Marian Evans [George Eliot] (London, 1854, and New York, 1957), p. 26). Marx's Feuerbachian views on this point will be examined in chapter 5.

[9] *God and the State*, p. 28.

called "divine" morality with what he called "human" (or "humane") morality. The former, which is the "absolute negation" of the latter, is based upon "respect for authority" and "contempt for humanity"; the latter is based upon "contempt for authority" and "respect for freedom and humanity." For Bakunin, "the tame dog imploring his master for a . . . glance" is the image of "a man kneeling before his God."[10]

Bakunin proposed that the "divine cult" (i.e., worship of God) be replaced by "respect for man (*respect humain*)."[11] The assertion of such respect is equivalent to the establishment of freedom. And this requires a dual revolt: a revolt against God ("the supreme phantom of theology") and a revolt against human tyranny.[12]

Bakunin saw religion not just as slavery but also as cruelty inflicted by the clergy and the church hierarchy upon ordinary people. The God of both Jews and Christians, he insists, is "atrociously jealous, vain, selfish, and blood-thirsty." All of the "blood shed in the name of religion from the beginning of history and the millions of human victims sacrificed for the greater glory of God" bear witness to the fact that natural human affection and solidarity, as soon as they are transformed into "divine love and religious charity," become the "scourge of mankind." Even the gentlest and most humane priests, Bakunin adds—anticipating Nietzsche—"always have at the bottom of their hearts . . . something cruel and bloody." Hence, for example, they regularly defend capital punishment.[13]

Like Proudhon, from whom he took many of his anarchist doctrines, Bakunin was anti-authoritarian in general and anti-

[10] Fédéralisme," in *Oeuvres*, 1:103.
[11] "Réponse," in *Oeuvres*, 6:125.
[12] *God and the State*, p. 13.
[13] "Fédéralisme," in *Oeuvres*, 1:115, 132 f., 66 f.

political in particular. He proposed to replace coercive socio-political institutions, including state and church, with uncoercive socio-economic institutions. Bakunin summoned men to "organize a new world, the world of human solidarity, on the ruins of all Churches and of all States."[14] He considered state and church inseparable, twin bastions of human slavery. ". . . slaves of God, [men] must also be slaves of the Church and the state, insofar as the latter is consecrated by the Church." All governments and all politicians stoutly defend religion, Bakunin declared, "so long as it teaches, as all [religions] do in any case, patience, resignation, and submission."[15] "There is not," Bakunin concluded, "there cannot be, a State without religion."[16]

Bakunin made no distinction between primitive Christianity (which Kropotkin, for example, praised as embodying the anarcho-socialist virtues of freedom, equality, and solidarity) and the nineteenth-century churches. He would, presumably, have argued that even the least institutionalized Christian community was based on the false and immoral principle that "since God exists, man is a slave."

According to Bakunin, states operate on the same assumption about human nature as do churches—the assumption, namely, that "natural man" is evil and hence must be curbed by force or the threat of force.[17] As an anarchist, Bakunin of course assumed with Rousseau that, on the contrary, men are—until corrupted

---

[14] La Commune de Paris et la notion de l'État (Paris, 1899), trans. Mary-Barbara Zeldin, in James M. Edie, James P. Scanlan, Mary-Barbara Zeldin, and George L. Kline, eds., Russian Philosophy (Chicago: Quadrangle Books, 1965), 1:408.

[15] "Fédéralisme," in Oeuvres, 1:63, 65.

[16] God and the State, p. 84.

[17] "Aux Compagnons de l'Association Internationale des Travailleurs," Letter no. 4, in Oeuvres, 1:224. Church and state alike, Bakunin declares, consider it "necessary to sacrifice human freedom in order to make men

by bad institutions—fundamentally good. But if men are "good" in Bakunin's sense—that is, sociable, cooperative, and altruistic —so that political sanctions are superfluous for maintaining order and harmony among them, it is difficult to see how "corrupting" political and ecclesiastical institutions ever became established. Or, once established—perhaps by some historical accident—how they managed to survive and grow.

Bakunin seems peculiarly insensitive to such difficulties. Instead of trying to meet them he retreats into endless reiteration of his charge that church and state are alike evil, and alike dispensable. The state is to be replaced by a "simple [i.e., nonpolitical] administration of public affairs (*affairs communes*)."[18] Apparently Bakunin, like Rousseau, is thinking of the tiny *res publica* of Geneva (or Bern) rather than the middle-sized *res publica* of France or the huge *res publica* of Russia. An "administration" that could cope with the *res publica* or *affairs communes* of either France or Russia would seem *prima facie* neither "simple" nor non-political.

Bakunin, of course, does not envisage any replacement for the church as an institution.

Bakunin was close to Marx, and even closer to Lenin, in his view of the socio-political function of religion in an "exploitative" society and in his strategy for eliminating this function. "So long as the masses of the people," he declared, echoing both Marx and the *philosophes*, "are sunk in religious superstition, they will always serve as a tool in the hands of all the despotisms allied against the liberation of mankind."[19]

---

moral and to transform them—according to the one, into saints—according to the other, into virtuous citizens" ("Fédéralisme," in *Oeuvres*, 1:160 [italics removed]).

[18] "Circulaire à mes amis d'Italie," in *Oeuvres*, 6:345.

[19] "Fédéralisme," in *Oeuvres*, 1:67 f.

Anticipating Lenin's criticism of Plekhanov nearly a generation later, Bakunin insists that "the propaganda of free thought"
will not be sufficient to erase religion from the minds of the
masses. People go to church, as they go to taverns, "to stupefy
themselves, to forget their misery." But "give them a human
existence, and they will no longer frequent either taverns or
churches. And it is only the social revolution that must and
will provide them with such an existence."[20]

What Lenin added was no more than the explicit statement
of a point clearly implicit in Bakunin; namely, that the struggle
against religion is part and parcel of the general class struggle.
We shall look more closely at Lenin's position in chapter 5.

II

Tolstoy's thought, like Bakunin's, was marked by maximalism
and one-sidedness. His philosophical and religious position has
been aptly characterized as a "tyranny of ethics."[21] I assume in
this section that the outlines of his life and work are well known.

Born in 1828, fourteen years after Bakunin, Tolstoy was
already a world-renowned novelist when, in the late 1870's, he
underwent a religious crisis. The fruit of this crisis was the sear-
ing manifesto of his Confession (written in 1879), followed by
such moral and religious tracts as What I Believe (1884), On
Life (1887), The Kingdom of God Is within You (1893), What
Is the Essence of Religion? (1902), and, finally, The Law of
Violence and the Law of Love (1908).[22]

[20] "Circulaire," in Oeuvres, 6:399.
[21] V. V. Zenkovsky, A History of Russian Philosophy, trans. George L.
Kline (London: Routledge & Kegan Paul; New York: Columbia University
Press, 1953), p. 392.
[22] A useful though mistitled compilation of Tolstoyana religiosa is Lift
Up Your Eyes: The Religious Writings of Leo Tolstoy, intro. by Stanley
R. Hopper (New York, 1960).

One major theme and two minor themes appear to have converged in precipitating Tolstoy's spiritual crisis: the theme of death and the themes of violence and secular culture (I shall return to the last two presently). In 1857 Tolstoy had witnessed a guillotining in Paris and the event had left an indelible impression. ". . . if a man were to be torn to pieces before my eyes," he wrote to a friend, "that would not be so repulsive as this efficient and elegant machine by means of which a powerful, fresh, and healthy human being was instantly killed."[23] Here, of course, the theme of death is interwoven with the theme of violence.

In 1860 Tolstoy's beloved older brother Nicholas died, not by violence but slowly and painfully, wasted by disease. Tolstoy was plunged into severe depression; and depression recurred with greater intensity in the late 1870's when two of his young children died.

Tolstoy now saw life as drained of all meaning by the inevitability of death. On at least one occasion he contemplated suicide. Stories like "Lucerne" express an intense, almost obsessive, longing for physical immortality and an almost pathological fear of death. Tolstoy never wholly overcame this fear. Gorky, who knew him well around 1900, reports that Tolstoy conveyed a sense of moral outrage that he, Leo Tolstoy, a writer of genius, should have been "condemned to die."[24]

After his "conversion" Tolstoy turned toward asceticism (he had been quite profligate as a young man) and assumed an attitude of indifference, even contempt, for what he called "material life."[25] Here the influence of Schopenhauer, whom Tolstoy

[23] Letter to V. P. Botkin, written in Paris, April 5, 1857, in L. N. Tolstoy, *Polnoye sobraniye sochineni* [Complete Works] (Moscow, 1949), 60:167 (In the remainder of this chapter referred to as *Sochineniya*).

[24] Maxim Gorky, *Reminiscences of Tolstoy, Chekhov, and Andreyev*, trans. S. S. Koteliansky and Leonard Woolf (New York, 1959), p. 31.

[25] One critic has referred to Tolstoy's "triple fear"—his fear of doubt, of

considered "the greatest genius among men,"[26] and of Buddhism are both apparent. Man's biological, social, and cultural existence is only *maya*—a veil of illusion, empty of value.

When in 1910, the last year of Tolstoy's life, the appearance of Halley's comet touched off widespread speculation about the possible destruction of all life on earth, either through direct collision or from exposure to the "lethal gases" of the comet's tail, Tolstoy wrote:

The thought that the comet might hook onto the earth and destroy it was very agreeable to me. Why shouldn't we admit this possibility? And, having admitted it, we see with special clarity that all the material consequences, the visible, tangible consequences of our activity in the material world, are nothing. Spiritual life can no more be disturbed by the destruction of the earth than the life of the universe by the death of a fly.[27]

In this same mood ten years earlier, Tolstoy had urged Gorky to study the Buddhist scriptures, assuring him that holiness could be achieved only by "subduing the will to live." Gorky quotes Tolstoy as exclaiming: "That's all nonsense, our earthly life."[28]

From the beginning, Tolstoy defined religion in deliberately

---

the flesh, and of death (Janko Lavrin, *Tolstoy, An Approach* [New York, 1946], p. 97).

[26] Letter to A. A. Fet, August 30, 1869, in *Sochineniya* (Moscow, 1953), 61:219. Eighteen years later, however, Tolstoy saw in Schopenhauer no more than a "talented scribbler" (*talantlivy pachkun*). See letter to N. N. Strakhov, October 16, 1887, in *ibid.*, 64:105.

[27] Letter to N. N. Gusev, January 14, 1910, in *Sochineniya* (Moscow, 1956), 81:44. For the "insignificance" of "sufferings and death in this life," see Tolstoy's 1902 article, "Chto takoye religiya, i v chem sushchnost yeyo?" [What Is Religion and What Is Its Essence?] as abridged in S. L. Frank, ed., *Antologiya russkoi filosofskoi mysli* [An Anthology of Russian Philosophic Thought] (New York, 1965), p. 45. The complete English translation is in *Lift Up Your Eyes*, pp. 267–314; this passage is from p. 314.

[28] *Reminiscences of Tolstoy*, pp. 5, 29.

general terms as "the establishment (*ustanovleniye*) of a man's relation to that whole [or "infinite being" or "infinite existence"] of which he feels himself to be a part, and from which he derives a guide (*rukovodstvo*) for his conduct."[29] Serving as a "guide for conduct" or "guide to life" is clearly an integral function of religion as Tolstoy conceived it.

As a young officer on duty during the Crimean War he had confided to his diary the "stupendous idea" of "founding a new religion . . ., Christianity, but purged of dogmas and mysticism. . . . Deliberately to promote the union of mankind by religion—that is the basic thought which, I hope, will dominate me."[30] Although he identified the "true religion" with Christianity, Tolstoy clearly intended a purified, non-denominational "Christianity," neither Protestant, nor Catholic, nor Orthodox. Indeed, he used language reminiscent of Bakunin in attacking "religious deception" and the "irrationality" and "absurdity" of received Christian dogma, specifically including the Trinity, the Resurrection, and the immortality of the soul. Anything miraculous or supernatural was repudiated in the name of what Tolstoy called "rational consciousness" (*razumnoye soznaniye*).

Tolstoy's "true religion" is made up of the "fundamental principles" shared by all the great religions, despite their external differences. These shared principles are extremely general: the belief that God is the "beginning and principle of all things (*nachalo vsevo*)," the morality of the Golden Rule, the ethics of non-violence, and so on.[31]

Here, as elsewhere, Tolstoy saw religion primarily as a foundation for morality—for an anarchist-pacifist morality of *ahimsa*

[29] "Chto takoye religiya?" pp. 25, 26, and *Lift Up Your Eyes*, pp. 272, 273.
[30] Quoted in Lavrin, *Tolstoy, An Approach*, p. 93.
[31] "Chto takoye religiya?" pp. 39 f and *Lift Up Your Eyes*, pp. 306 f.

(absolute non-action or non-violence, since, in the Buddhist view, all action involves violence). The influence of Schopenhauer and Buddhism here merges with that of Rousseau.

When, as a young man, Tolstoy had broken with the faith of his fathers he had replaced the crucifix on the chain around his neck with a miniature portrait of Rousseau, probably in imitation of Julien Sorel in The Red and the Black, who wore a portrait of Napoleon. Tolstoy may be said to have moved from an early and quite orthodox Rousseauism to a final, "revisionist" neo-Rousseauism. In the beginning he held, with Rousseau, that men are good and institutions bad; in the end he held that institutions are bad, men aren't very good, and institutions can be improved only by reforming men's hearts—or, in his own jargon, by raising them from subjugation to the "law of violence" and bringing them under the sway of the "law of love." However—as an early Russian Marxist critic of Tolstoy pointed out—according to Rousseau man's "divine nature" demands a just social order, whereas in Tolstoy's view man's "divine nature" demands a renunciation of all "material" (including social and political) life. Rousseau would retain the state but make it serve individual citizens; Tolstoy preached the absolute negation of the state.[32]

Tolstoy sought systematic support in the New Testament for his principle of absolute non-violence, and especially in the Sermon on the Mount. He was fond of quoting Christ's admonition: "Resist not evil; but whosoever shall smite thee on thy right cheek, turn to him the other also" (Matt. 5:39). But it was the doctrine itself, not its scriptural source, that he prized

[32] Esther Luba Axelrod, Tolstois Weltanschauung and ihre Entwickelung (Stuttgart, 1902), p. 71. Axelrod, who wrote in Russian under the pseudonym "Ortodoks," presented her study of Tolstoy as a doctoral dissertation at the University of Bern.

and defended. In 1899 Tolstoy welcomed the skeptical conclusions of one of the German "higher critics" about the existence of the "historical Jesus" as showing that New Testament ethics comes not "from one temporary and local source, but from the totality of the spiritual life of mankind."[33] Earlier he had declared confidently that "if there had been neither Christ nor His teaching, I would have discovered this truth [of the "law of love"] myself."[34]

Opposed to the New Testament exhortation to "love one another" and "turn the other cheek" there is, of course, the forceful driving of the money-changers from the temple and the hard saying "I bring not peace but a sword." Tolstoy's "rational consciousness" had no patience with such sayings. He studied Greek and published his own edition of the New Testament, severely edited to eliminate, or explain away, anything that could suggest a Christian sanction for the use of force under any circumstances whatever.[35]

The principle of Tolstoyan non-violence precludes the doing of any social good that involves the application of physical force. As Tolstoy would have put it, the use of force against human beings is itself an absolute evil and thus is always worse than the relative evil against which it is turned. Nothing accomplished through violence can be good; the alleged good end will always be tainted by the violent means used to achieve it.

[33] Letter to P. I. Biryukov, August 1, 1899, in *Sochineniya* (Moscow-Leningrad, 1933), 72:164. The book in question is S. G. Verus' *Vergleichende Übersicht der vier Evangelien* (Leipzig, 1897).

[34] Letter to M. A. Engelhardt, December 20(?), 1882, in *Sochineniya* (Moscow-Leningrad, 1934), 63:116. The English version is in *Tolstoy Centenary Edition*, trans. Aylmer Maude (London, 1934), 14:379.

[35] In conversation with Konstantin Leontyev at the Optina Pustyn monastery in 1890, Tolstoy referred to "my Gospel" (*moyo Yevangeliye*); Leontyev was furious. Reported by V. V. Rozanov in *Okolo tserkovnykh sten* [By the Walls of the Church] (St. Petersburg, 1906), 2:116.

In the extreme case of refusal to use force even to restrain a person criminally insane, "I run the risk," Tolstoy insists, "only of my death, or *the death of other men who can be killed by the madman;* . . . and death in fulfilling the will of God is a blessing. . . . [But by resorting to force] I run the risk of acting quite contrary to the law of Christ—which is worse than death."[36]

A later statement of Tolstoy seems at first glance to contradict the inclusion (in the italicized phrase of the passage just quoted) of the lives of other men in the range of what the non-resister may rightfully risk. "A man's conscience," he wrote, "may demand the sacrifice of his own life [but] not the life of another." In fact, however, Tolstoy means by "other" not the possible victim or victims of the madman's or criminal's violence but the madman or criminal himself. Tolstoy considered it immoral to attempt forcibly to defend anyone—however "weak and defenseless"—against anyone else's threatened violence. He insisted that it is impossible ever to know which will be the greater evil: the defender's violence or that which the defender wishes to prevent. He put the point vividly:

The villain raises a knife over his victim; I have a pistol in my hand and can kill him. But I really do not know, and cannot know, whether the upraised knife will effect its evil purpose. It may not, while I most likely shall accomplish my evil [sic!] deed.[37]

Tolstoy sometimes appealed to the distinction between man's "animal personality" or "animal self" (*zhivotnaya lichnost*), with its merely "empirical consciousness," and his true, unified "rational consciousness," to try to mitigate the paradoxical

[36] Letter to Adin Ballou, February 21–24, 1890, in *Sochineniya* (Moscow, 1953), 65:35 (the original was in English).

[37] *The Law of Violence and the Law of Love*, trans. James P. Scanlan, in *Russian Philosophy*, 2:231.

thrust of his doctrine of non-violent resistance to evil.[38] But the distinction doesn't really help: If Tolstoy claims that only the contemptible animal self of the victim or the observer is being risked, one must point out that, likewise, only the contemptible animal self of the madman or criminal is being risked. And if Tolstoy claims that the precious "rational consciousness" is involved on one side we must point out that the equally precious "rational consciousnesses" of the others are equally involved.

Tolstoy's condemnation of the "animal self" is a corollary not only of his asceticism (to gratify that self, he insists, is to experience a "continuous dying") but also of his impersonalism.[39] Only the animal self is individual or personal; the rational consciousness is supra-individual or impersonal. Asceticism and impersonalism, decidedly Schopenhauerian-Buddhist in tone, come together in Tolstoy's fulminations against eros as both individual (or personal) and "animal." True Christian agapē, he maintains, is both impersonal and spiritual.

The preaching of impersonalism and non-violence lies at the heart of Tolstoy's "true religion." His position is clearly an ethical one, but it is doubtfully religious and perhaps—like Buddhism—is compatible with atheism. Shestov had seen this in 1900 when he charged Tolstoy with "deliberately substituting the good for God, and brotherly love for the good." Shestov even suggested that Tolstoy's moralistic formula "God is the good" was, in the last analysis, equivalent to Nietzsche's nihilistic formula "God is dead." Shestov also commented acidly on

[38] See "O zhizni" [On Life], Sochineniya, 26:363 ff, 368, 383.

[39] As Janko Lavrin reminds us, Tolstoy warmly welcomed Pascal's harsh saying "le moi est haïssable" (Tolstoy, An Approach, p. 101). Tolstoy himself declared that "life as individual existence has been outlived by mankind," Sochineniya, 26:380.

Tolstoy's rather simple-minded optimism, his belief that if one merely presses down on the "Archimedean lever" of absolute non-violence, the "entire old world will turn over, all evils will disappear, and people will become happy."[40]

Non-violence for Tolstoy seems to have been a means of "spiritual self-perfection" and a gateway to nirvana—the extinction of will and desire. Tolstoy once confessed his own "religious reverence for—and terror of—Nirvana," adding that nothing could be more important than the nothingness of nirvana and that he found it "much more interesting than life."[41]

Whatever we may make of this last statement, it is clear that for Tolstoy non-violence was not a means of social or political action. Unlike Gandhi, who was his disciple only in some limited respects, Tolstoy would not, I think, approve of even the most "non-violent" current civil rights demonstrations. He would disapprove of them because they are organized, because they may and often do lead to violence, and finally because civil rights accrue to human individuals under a rule of law. For Tolstoy, no human individual (as "animal self") is ultimately very important, and every rule of law is at bottom a rule of violence. As one critic put it, Tolstoy "refused to see any difference between law and violence, between functional authority and oppression."[42]

Older anarchists, like Proudhon (whom Tolstoy had met in Brussels in 1860) and Bakunin, were equally insensitive to such distinctions. But Tolstoy went beyond both of his predecessors, and beyond his contemporary Kropotkin, in the inclusiveness

[40] *Dobro v uchenii Gr. Tolstovo i F. Nitshe* [The Good in the Teaching of Count Tolstoy and F. Nietzsche] (St. Petersburg, 1900), pp. 98, 100, 39.

[41] Letter to A. A. Fet, January 30, 1873, in *Sochineniya* (Moscow, 1953), 62:7. (This passage is quoted in Lavrin, *Tolstoy, An Approach* [p. 88], who wrongly dates the letter January, 1872.)

[42] Lavrin, *Tolstoy, An Approach*, pp. 107 f.

29

of his anarchism. He was not only a social and political anarchist, he was also a cultural anarchist who could flatly proclaim "*Fiat justitia, pereat cultura.*"[43]

He rejected the church no more and no less than the state, law, armies, prisons, police forces, art, science, technology. He sharply attacked ecclesiastical support of military conscription and the religious sanction of war and capital punishment—this last was a point of contact with Bakunin. He also castigated the "utter madness" of "using the brief interval . . . between birth and death to make speeches in parliaments or at congresses of socialist comrades; to judge [one's] neighbors in courts, seize them, lock them up, and murder them; or throw bombs at them" (a reference to Bakuninite revolutionary anarchists).[44]

That scientists, and even theologians, could not tell men "how they should live" came as a great shock to Tolstoy; he described the trauma vividly in his *Confession*. Science, he concluded, is for the most part either useless or positively harmful. The natural sciences, through their applications in technology, are employed by the ruling classes (Tolstoy frequently used the expression *pravyashchiye klassy*, echoing both Marx and Bakunin) to oppress the masses. The social sciences, as well as speculative philosophy and theology, serve to justify this exploitative order.[45]

In his later years Tolstoy expressed a cordial hatred of technology—trains, automobiles, electric power. Men, he insisted, should ride horseback and till the earth with wooden plows. As for the "miracles" of modern transportation and communication,

[43] Tolstoy, *The Slavery of Our Time*; quoted in Lavrin, *Tolstoy, An Approach*, p. 110.

[44] *The Law of Violence*, p. 228.

[45] Tolstoy, like other Russians of the period, used the term 'science' (*nauka*) in the broad sense of the German *Wissenschaft*, to include such intellectual disciplines as history, philosophy, and theology.

We may keep on inventing new submarine, subterranean, aerial, and superaerial contraptions for transporting people from place to place with the utmost speed, and new devices for broadcasting their words and thoughts; but the people thus transported are unwilling, unqualified, and unable to do anything but evil, and their broadcast words and thoughts can do nothing but incite men to evil.[46]

Tolstoy hated the city, partly because it was the center from which technology and mechanization spread to the countryside, partly for the reasons that made Rousseau hate Paris: its bigness and the violence, hypocrisy, and artificiality of its inhabitants. But Tolstoy also hated the city for its squalor and ugliness— not just Paris, Petersburg, and Moscow but also, and perhaps especially, Tula: the city nearest his country estate of Yasnaya Polyana ("Clear Glade") and site of the famous munitions works that were among the first industrial enterprises in Imperial Russia. Yasnaya Polyana is, and was, a rural idyll of rolling fields, woods, rivers, ponds, and teeming wildlife. Tula is, and presumably was in Tolstoy's day, about as ugly and squalid a factory slum as one could imagine.[47]

Tolstoy agreed with Bakunin that the historical churches have fostered inequality, hierarchy, and discord among men. He even used one of Bakunin's favorite terms, odureniye=stupéfaction, to describe the psychological condition of ordinary believers. They live, he said, "in that stupefied condition (v tom odurennom sostoyanii) in which the clergy and the government keep them."[48] And he echoed Bakunin's charge—and Voltaire's—

---

[46] The Law of Violence, p. 216. In Leontyev we shall see a similarly drastic rejection of technology, but one that is aesthetically and religiously rather than morally motivated (pp. 45–46 below).

[47] I base this observation on my visits to Tula and Yasnaya Polyana in 1956 and 1960.

[48] "Chto takoye religiya?" pp. 43 f and Lift Up Your Eyes, p. 312.

that the "history of the Church" is a "history of cruelty and horror."

But Tolstoy insisted that *true* religion brings men together in harmony—just as true Christianity teaches that all men are equal because all are equally insignificant in relation to the Infinite. The only good thing that Bakunin had found to say about Christianity was that Christ was a "friend and consoler of the wretched, of the ignorant, of the slaves," whose teaching was the occasion for the "first intellectual revolt of the proletariat."[49]

Tolstoy agreed with Bakunin in opposing whatever he considered "irrational."[50] But, of course, Bakunin considered *all* religions irrational whereas Tolstoy felt that the irrationality of the historical religions could be purged away in a "true religion" that was perfectly rational.

Berdyaev saw in this enlightenment optimism, this faith in the efficacy of "rational consciousness," a chief defect of Tolstoy's religious teaching. Tolstoy, he said, was insensitive both to the power of evil in the world and to the fact of tragedy. ". . . he imagined the source of wickedness to be in the consciousness instead of in the will and its freedom."[51] Berdyaev considered Tolstoy's position a non-Christian "abstract moralism," which sees Christ not as a redeemer but as a moral teacher and lawgiver, and ignores the mystical aspects of Christianity.

For Berdyaev himself, as we shall see in chapter 3, the morality of love is incompatible with the morality of law. Thus

---

[49] *God and the State*, p. 75; reprinted in *Russian Philosophy*, 1:421.

[50] Cf. their parallel rejections of Tertullian's *Credo quia absurdum* (in *God and the State*, pp. 15, 77; "What Is Religion?" in *Lift Up Your Eyes*, p. 283).

[51] Berdyaev, "The Worth of Christianity and the Unworthiness of Christians," trans. Donald Attwater, in *The Bourgeois Mind and Other Essays* (London and New York, 1934), p. 122.

Tolstoy's "law of love" is a contradiction in terms. In fact, Berdyaev asserts, love became for Tolstoy "a law without grace, a source of indictment." Tolstoy indicted other men as immoral "because they did not renounce their private property, because they did not work with their hands, because they ate meat and smoked tobacco."[52]

Another critic charged Tolstoy with attempting to force men into the community of brotherly love, replacing the unsubtle coercion of political and legal systems with the subtle coercion of the "law of love," understood as a "coercive general norm."

Do not kill under any circumstances, do not use force against any man . . . , do not eat meat, do not smoke, . . . —with this network of "don'ts" Tolstoy not only pitilessly seizes and binds the whole of human life; he also regards this binding as the adequate, completely valid elaboration of the Christian commandment of love.[53]

It seems clear, both from the testimony of those who knew him and from the merciless self-analysis of his diaries, that Tolstoy was by nature despotic and dictatorial, eager to convert others to his views through sheer force of logic. As Gorky said, "He liked to compel [people], to compel them to read, walk, be vegetarians, love the peasants, and believe in the infallibility of the rational-religious reflections of Leo Tolstoy."[54]

In several respects Bakunin and Tolstoy, despite their differences, set precedents that were taken up by Lenin and ultimately by the Soviet anti-religionists. Bakunin, perhaps even more than Marx, bequeathed to the Leninists a militancy and

---

[52] *Ibid.*, p. 123. As early as 1900 Shestov had pointed out that Tolstoy systematically intimidated people, treating resistance to the least detail of his teaching as immoral (*Dobro v uchenii*, p. 39).

[53] S. L. Frank, "Leo Tolstoy als Denker und Dichter," *Zeitschrift für slavische Philologie*, 10 (1933): 74 f.

[54] *Reminiscences of Tolstoy*, p. 34.

33

vehemence of anti-religious statement and an insistence that "propaganda is not enough"—that the struggle against religion is an integral part of the class struggle both because religious institutions have a vested interest in the status quo and because religious belief functions as an opiate for individual believers.

Tolstoy intellectualized religion, reducing it to a "rational rule of conduct." This narrowing was continued and increased by Soviet anti-religionists. Following Plekhanov, they treated religion as a kind of science but, of course, as "bad" science, "pseudo-science," to be "refuted" by confrontation with "good" science. Soviet propagandists agreed with Tolstoy that religion and morality are closely connected; they of course disagreed with him, as Bakunin would have done, on the acceptability of both religion and religiously based morality. The dispute, however, was carried on largely in the intellectualistic conceptual terms that Tolstoy himself had adopted.

Leontyev and Rozanov, Tolstoy's contemporaries to whom we turn in chapter 2, were at pains to reject his intellectualism as well as his impersonalism and anarchism. Leontyev specifically criticized Tolstoy's "true Christianity" as wishy-washy and "rose-colored." Understandably, both Leontyev and Rozanov considered Bakunin's atheism, socialism, and anarchism beneath critical contempt.

2

RELIGIOUS NEO-CONSERVATIVES:
LEONTYEV AND ROZANOV

Despite the similarity of many of their views and the quarter-
century overlap in the periods of their intellectual maturity
(ca. 1851 to 1876), Bakunin and Tolstoy never met and they
exchanged no letters. In contrast, Leontyev and Rozanov,
although they did not meet, carried on a cordial and lively cor-
respondence during the last year of Leontyev's life (1891).
Rozanov, twenty-five years younger than Leontyev, survived him
by twenty-eight years.

Leontyev and Rozanov were drawn together by their common
opposition to most of the received notions of West European
and Russian intellectual life in the late nineteenth century: faith
in the reality of historical progress and the efficacy of science,
technology, and "progressive" political programs—whether radical or liberal. Both of them repudiated Bakunin's "ethical" or
pseudo-ethical grounding of atheism, and both of them scorned
Bakunin's positivism and anarcho-socialism.

Leontyev and Rozanov have both been called "Russian
Nietzsches." Their style of writing, like that of their younger
contemporary, Shestov, is aphoristic, sporadically brilliant, often
vehement, almost always polemical, and in this sense "Nie-

tzschean."[1] Both of them shared Nietzche's rejection of conventional "bourgeois" values, although in Rozanov's case this rejection did not extend to the values of domesticity, of "hearth and home."

On substantive issues Leontyev was generally much closer to Nietzsche than was Rozanov. A Nietzschean *avant la lettre*, Leontyev stressed the "aesthetic," but with a subtle difference. Leontyev meant primarily the "aesthetics of daily life"; Nietzsche meant the "aesthetics of fine art and high culture."[2]

Leontyev and Rozanov reacted in detail to the Tolstoyan position which we considered in chapter 1. Both men repudiated Tolstoy's reduction of religion to ethics and of ethics to non-violence. However, their attitudes toward Tolstoy's position, though equally negative, were by no means identical. Leontyev rejected what he considered the "rose-colored sentimentality" of Tolstoy's religious teaching. Rozanov challenged the asceticism of Tolstoy's later sexual morality.

These differences are reflected in the positive values which Leontyev and Rozanov opposed to Tolstoyan Christianity. In Leontyev's case it was aestheticism, followed in his later years (after his religious crisis of 1869–71) by a "black" religiousness of Byzantine severity. In Rozanov's case it was a kind of biological mysticism, a metaphysics of sex and family life. Tolstoy's

[1] Rozanov characterized Leontyev's style as "nervous and sharp, passionate and poignant" (V. V. Rozanov, "Neuznanny fenomen" [An Unrecognized Phenomenon], in *Pamyati Konstantina Nikolayevicha Leontyeva: Literaturny sbornik* [St. Petersburg, 1911]; reprinted with Leontyev's *Analiz, stil i veyaniye: O romanakh gr. L. N. Tolstovo* [Analysis, Style, and Atmosphere: On the Novels of Count L. N. Tolstoy] [1890], in Brown University Slavic Reprint no. 3 [Providence, R.I., 1965]. Page references will be to this reprint. The passage in question is on p. 146).

[2] Rozanov said that when he first read about Nietzsche (in an article published in a Moscow philosophy journal in 1892) he exclaimed "Yes, that is Leontyev—no difference whatever" ("Neuznanny fenomen," pp. 155 f).

religious position centered on brotherly love (agapē); Rozanov's stressed sexual love (eros); Leontyev's emphasized the fear of God (phobos).

I

Konstantin Nikolayevich Leontyev was born in 1831, just three years after Tolstoy. He came from a family of landowning gentry. His pious mother imbued him with an early love of beauty and a respect for strict discipline. Leontyev studied first at a provincial gymnasium and then at the Faculty of Medicine of Moscow University (the choice of medicine seems to have been his mother's rather than his own). The exigencies of the Crimean War prevented him from completing the last year of medical school, and he was sent to the Crimea as a medical technician (lekar). His first short story had appeared in 1851, when he was just twenty, and this and other early stories impressed Turgenev, who helped the young writer with advice and money.

After his discharge from military service Leontyev became house physician to a family of the landed gentry near Moscow and devoted his leisure time to writing. He was not happy in this position, and within two years he moved to St. Petersburg, where he established himself as a writer, giving up the practice of medicine altogether. In 1861 he married a beautiful but uneducated Greek woman of humble origin, who later (in 1867) became mentally ill. Leontyev published two novels, in 1861 and 1864.

In 1863 he entered the Russian diplomatic service and spent the next eight years as a consular official in various parts of the Turkish Empire, including the island of Crete and the cities of Salonika (Thessalonika), Constantinople (Istanbul), and Adrianople (Edirne). He was much attracted by the life and

37

culture of the Middle East, both Greek and Turkish, and by the two dominant religions: Greek Orthodoxy and Islam.[3] The frequency of Leontyev's extramarital adventures with Greek, Turkish, and Bulgarian women during this period seems to have contributed to his wife's mental breakdown.[4]

Leontyev was extremely handsome, in a semi-oriental way, and slightly effeminate. According to some commentators, Leontyev's mother raised him "rather like a girl." Psychologically he was "bisexual, masculine-feminine."[5] Here the term 'bisexual' (dvupoly) is probably not meant in the current English sense of "both heterosexual and homosexual"; however, as I have mentioned, there were rumors about Leontyev's "bisexuality" in the current sense of the term. If he was in fact "latently homosexual," his early upbringing, combined with the Greco-Turkish milieu in which he spent so many years, may have made manifest what had been latent.

Toward the end of his period of diplomatic service, in 1869 and continuing through 1871, Leontyev underwent a profound spiritual crisis, resulting in what he called a "personal" conver-

[3] Rozanov noted that Leontyev was the first Russian, and perhaps the first European, to appreciate the specific values of "Turkishness," including militancy, religious fanaticism, fidelity to God, and "a peculiar respect for man" ("Neuznanny fenomen," p. 151).

[4] Cf. N. A. Berdyaev, Konstantin Leontyev: Ocherk iz istorii russkoi religioznoi mysli [Konstantin Leontyev: An Essay in the History of Russian Religious Thought] (Paris, 1926), p. 49; trans. George Reavey (London, 1940).

[5] Berdyaev, Konstantin Leontyev, p. 21. Rozanov was quite explicit about Leontyev's homosexuality but he made it clear that he did not consider it "immoral." He noted that this characteristic placed Leontyev in the company of other "men of genius": the "leaders, lawgivers, and prophets" of mankind, including Socrates, Plato, Raphael, Michelangelo, Da Vinci, and Shakespeare. See Rozanov's commentary on a letter from Strakhov, dated April 22, 1892, in Literaturnyie izgnanniki [Literary Exiles] (1913), 1:325n., 326n.; reprinted in V. V. Rozanov, Izbrannoye [Selected Works], ed. Yu. Ivask (New York, 1956), p. 184.

sion to Byzantine Christianity. He resigned his diplomatic post, but before his resignation became effective (in 1873) he spent a year (1870–71) living on Mt. Athos, the rugged and rocky peninsula on the Greek coast which was, and is, the site of a cluster of Greek Orthodox monasteries noted for the asceticism and severity of their spiritual discipline.

When Leontyev returned to Russia his political views were already conservative, even reactionary, but he was an original and imaginative "neo-conservative" who found the conventional and stolid reactionary circles of St. Petersburg almost unbearable.[6] He served for a time as an official censor of literature in Moscow, but gave this up, and in 1887 he took the drastic step of officially divorcing his wife in order to withdraw to the Optina Pustyn, one of Russia's most famous monasteries. The well-known *starets*, Ambrose, became his spiritual mentor.[7] In August of 1891 Leontyev secretly took monastic vows; in November of the same year he died.

Rozanov has said that Leontyev had neither predecessors nor followers, that he issued from no school of thought and founded none.[8] This is essentially true. Leontyev's views evoked almost no response, either in Russia or abroad, during his lifetime and very little after his death. His isolation and near-oblivion con-

[6] Leontyev's rejection of liberalism and secular egalitarianism dates from 1862. It was precipitated by a conversation in St. Petersburg with a follower of Chernyshevski, who defended the ideal of a future "housing development" in which everyone would live in identical, small, neat houses. Leontyev found the prospect intolerable. See Berdyaev, *Konstantin Leontyev*, pp. 35 f.

[7] The Russian term *starets* (literally "elder") connotes spiritual authority rather than age. Rozanov said that he shared Leontyev's "profound regard" for *starets* Ambrose ("Neuznanny fenomen," p. 140). It is generally assumed that *starets* Ambrose was the model, or at least a model, for *starets* Zosima in Dostoyevski's *Brothers Karamazov*.

[8] Rozanov, "Neuznanny fenomen," p. 148.

trast sharply with the noisy reputations of Bakunin and Tolstoy.

Leontyev, nevertheless, was a highly original and independent thinker. His "Nietzschean" views were formulated almost a decade before Nietzsche's first works appeared, and he died before Nietzsche's fame had spread to Russia. There is no direct influence of Western thinkers on his religious or ethical thought. He was, however, influenced, or at least stimulated, by several Russian thinkers: by Herzen (in formulating his anti-Philistine aestheticism), by Danilevski (in formulating his "organic" philosophy of history), and by Solovyov (in some of his religious views, although Leontyev came to differ sharply with Solovyov on important points).

Rozanov, who relates Leontyev's "aestheticism" to his "ultra-biological" striving for maximum intensity of life, sees both as rooted in an "anti-death instinct" (*anti-smertnost*) and a corollary belief in the "immortality of beauty." Berdyaev, who quotes Rozanov on this point, adds that Leontyev, after his religious crisis and despairing of the "ultra-biological," sought "personal salvation" (Leontyev's own term) from spiritual ruin, that is, damnation. The pre-conversion period was marked by an "aesthetic rapture over life," the post-conversion period by a "religious fear of destruction." But Leontyev's powerful "anti-death instinct" and his firm belief in the "immortality of beauty" pervaded *both* periods.[9]

That beauty is an "end in itself" and the only "true measure of all things" is a conviction expressed by Milkeyev, the hero of Leontyev's early (1864) novel, V *svoyom krayu* [Back at Home].[10] In a later, unfinished essay, bearing the characteristic

[9] Berdyaev, *Konstantin Leontyev*, p. 9.

[10] In K. N. Leontyev, *Sochineniya* [Works] (Moscow, 1912–1914), 1:304. Berdyaev called Leontyev the "first Russian aesthete," noting that he began to defend aesthetic values at a time (the early 1860's) when the

title "The Average European as an Ideal and Instrument of Universal Destruction," Leontyev added:

The aesthetic criterion is the most trustworthy and general, for it is uniquely applicable to all societies, to all religions, and to all epochs. What is beneficial to all of them—we do not know and never shall know. What is beautiful and elegant and lofty in them—it is high time we found out![11]

Like Nietzsche, Leontyev considered security, comfort, and "leveling equality" to be destructive of vitality and creativity. Leontyev's fictional hero is prepared to repudiate "impotence, lethargy, indifference, vulgarity and shopkeeper's cautiousness" and to celebrate risk, conflict, and even bloodshed. "Which is better," Milkeyev exclaims, "the bloody, but spiritually luxuriant period of the Renaissance or the tame, prosperous, moderate existence of contemporary Denmark, Holland, and Switzerland?"[12]

That social violence stimulates cultural creativity is a familiar theme among the French romanticists, and Leontyev probably found it there, but his hero Milkeyev goes on to ask an unromantic question which anticipates the late Tolstoy, and perhaps Leontyev's own post-conversion Orthodoxy: "What is so important about our mere physiological existence? It isn't worth a kopek!" He appends an extreme statement, motivated by what Leontyev was to call "aesthetic amoralism," which must have been profoundly shocking to the "men of the sixties": "*A single century-old magnificent tree is worth more than twenty faceless*

---

dominant (radical-nihilist) opinion was explicitly anti-aesthetic (*Konstantin Leontyev*, pp. 6 f).

[11] From abridged trans. of "Sredny Yevropeyets kak ideal i oruzhiye vseobshchevo razrusheniya" in *Sochineniya* (5:9–69), by William Shafer and George L. Kline, in *Russian Philosophy*, ed. James M. Edie, James P. Scanlan, Mary-Barbara Zeldin, and George L. Kline (Chicago: Quadrangle Books, 1965), 2:279. (This is the first translation into English of any work by Leontyev.)

[12] *Sochineniya*, 1:305, 414.

men; and I will not cut it down in order to be able to buy medicine for the peasants' cholera!"[13]

For the last thirty years of his life Leontyev was convinced that democratic-egalitarian "progress" meant the flattening out of diversity, the muting of contrast, and the erosion of beauty.[14] Human life, he insisted, should emulate nature, seeking complexity, richness, luxuriance, and variety of forms. "The chief element of variety," Milkeyev had said, "is the individual person, and he is higher than his works. The many-sided strength or the one-sided valor of the individual is, more than anything else, the clear goal of history."[15]

Looking to the historical past, Leontyev, like Herzen before him, saw a retrogression, a gradual grinding down of the individual brilliance and intensity of ancient and medieval times under the massive pressure of modern mediocrity, reinforced by the egalitarian drift of advanced technology.

Would it not be dreadful and offensive [Leontyev wrote in 1882] to think that Moses went up to Sinai, that the Greeks built their splendid Acropolises, the Romans waged their Punic wars, the handsome genius Alexander, in a plumed helmet, crossed the Granicus and fought at Arbela, that the apostles preached, martyrs suffered, poets sang, painters painted, and knights shone in the tourneys, only in order that the French, German, or Russian bourgeois, in his ugly and comical clothing, should sit complacently . . . upon the ruins of all this past greatness?[16]

Unlike Herzen, who knew only Russia and Western Europe, Leontyev also knew the Middle East. He saw in Greece, Turkey, and the Balkans a kind of society that in the 1860's and 1870's

[13] *Ibid.,* pp. 305 f., 306 (italics added).
[14] Rozanov wrote that Leontyev "died in agony, an agony that lasted for thirty years" ("Neuznanny fenomen," p. 139).
[15] V *svoyom krayu,* in *Sochineniya,* 1:414.
[16] "Pisma o vostochnykh delakh" [Letters on Eastern Affairs] (1882–83), in *Sochineniya,* 5:426 (italics removed).

was still untouched by European liberalism and modern technology, and thus still preserved its own colorful and exotic form of life.

Like Herzen after 1848, he saw no hope for Western Europe. The *mania democratica progressiva* had gone too far; the disease was incurable.[17] The "average European," who was "neither a peasant nor a gentleman, neither a soldier nor a priest, . . . neither a Tyrolian nor a Circassian, neither a Trappist in a hair shirt nor a prelate in brocade," but only "a self-satisfied caricature of former men," had won the day.[18] His black frock coat should be regarded as a sign of mourning for the artistic and religious greatness of Europe's dead past.

Leontyev developed a rather schematic and "biologistic" theory of history—inspired by Danilevski—to explain the decline of nineteenth-century European culture. Historical cultures, like living organisms, he claimed, develop from a state of "initial simplicity," pass through a process of isolating particularization to higher states of "flourishing complexity" (or "complex flowering"), and then sink, through "leveling interfusion" and "secondary simplification," to organic death.[19] According to Leontyev, European culture is far advanced in this terminal process, having reached the "flourishing complexity" of its prime during the high Middle Ages.

Contemporary European culture, Leontyev declared (following Herzen), is characterized by *meshchanstvo*—bourgeois-Philistine narrow-mindedness and vulgarity. He saw it in St.

[17] Leontyev used the Latin phrase in "Nashi novyie khristiane: II: O vsemirnoi lyubvi: Rech F. M. Dostoyevskovo na pushkinskom prazdnike" [Our New Christians: II: On Universal Love: F. M. Dostoyevski's Speech at the Pushkin Celebration] (1880), in *Sochineniya*, 8:203.

[18] "The Average European," in *Russian Philosophy*, 2:279.

[19] Cf. "Vizantizm i Slavyanstvo" [Byzantinism and Slavdom] (1875), in *Sochineniya*, 5:197.

Petersburg,[20] in "railroads, dinner jackets, top hats, rationalism," and in "machines, teachers, professors, lawyers, chemical laboratories, bourgeois luxury and bourgeois depravity, bourgeois moderation and bourgeois morality." These phenomena accompany the utopian striving for "universal equality, universal love, universal justice, and universal prosperity."[21] Vladimir Solovyov seems to have been right when he observed that Leontyev had no "ruling love" but only a "ruling hatred"—of contemporary European civilization.[22] Leontyev himself called it a "philosophical hatred" and admitted that it was a central motivation in all of his writing.

Leontyev considered social injustice and "the pressure of classes, despotism, danger, strong passions, prejudices, superstitions, fanaticism" essential to the "aesthetics" or "poetry" of life, as contrasted to its unaesthetic "prose."[23] All of the items in this rather miscellaneous catalogue, Leontyev would claim, involve or facilitate "unity in diversity" and the "despotism of form"—a despotism that is socio-political as well as aesthetic.[24]

Rozanov saw in Leontyev's conversion to a severe Byzantine

[20] St. Petersburg, which Peter the Great built to "open a window to the West," was traditionally considered the locus of West European culture, in contrast to Moscow, the locus of Byzantine-Slavic culture. The leading symbol of West European liberal-Philistine influence in Russia, for Leontyev, was the "St. Petersburg lawyer."

[21] "The Average European," in *Russian Philosophy*, 2:271, 280.

[22] V. S. Solovyov, "Pamyati K. N. Leontyeva" [In Memory of K. N. Leontyev], *Russkoye Obozreniye*, 1 (January, 1892): 353. Bulgakov referred to Leontyev's ruling hatred as a "miso-europeanism" (S. N. Bulgakov, "Pobeditel-Pobezhdyonny: Sudba K. N. Leontyeva" [Victor and Vanquished: The Fate of K. N. Leontyev] (1916), in *Tikhiye dumy* [Quiet Thoughts] (Moscow, 1918), p. 120).

[23] "Yeshcho o 'Dikare'" [Once More on the "Savage"] (1880), in *Sochineniya*, 8:98.

[24] Leontyev characterized form as "the despotism of an inner idea" (*Sochineniya*, 5: 197).

Christianity an attempt (1) to set a limit to his philosophical skepticism and pessimism and (2) to find a bulwark against the destructive leveling process of European liberalism and social-ism.[25] The second motivation seems especially clear in such passages as the following.

The universal destruction of monarchy, of the gentry, of mystical positive religions, of wars and inequality, would lead to a prosiness so dreadful that it is horrible even to imagine it.[26]

Leontyev saw no possibility of poetry in life "without the mysticism and plastic beauty of religion, without the mag-nificence and threatening power of the state, without a splen-did and firmly established aristocracy."[27] In another place he declared that in a society from which heroism, tragedy, even the "demonic" had been eliminated, religious energies would gradually "dry up."[28] "Religion in social life," he had written a decade earlier, "is like the heart in an animal organism. It is the *primum vivens, ultimum moriens* [i.e., the first to live and the last to die] of the nation."[29]

Leontyev was especially repelled by the "prose" of technology —the thought of "a gray, impersonal bourgeois or workers'

[25] Rozanov, "Neuznanny fenomen," p. 150.

[26] Leontyev, "Zapiski otshelnika: Dva grafa: Aleksei Vronski i Lev Tol-stoi" [Notes of a Recluse: Two Counts: Alexis Vronsky and Leo Tolstoy] (1888), in *Sochineniya*, 7:267.

[27] "Plody natsionalnykh dvizheni na Pravoslavnom Vostoke" [The Fruits of National Movements in the Orthodox East] (1888–89), in *Sochineniya*, 5:213. The first two phrases are extraordinarily concise and vivid in Russian: "Bez mistiki i plastiki religioznoi, bez velichavoi i groznoi gosudarstven-nosti."

[28] "Pisma k V. S. Solovyovu—O natsionalizme politicheskom i kultur-nom" [Letters to V. S. Solovyov—On Political and Cultural Nationalism] (1890), in *Sochineniya*, 6:283 f.

[29] Editorial in the Warsaw newspaper *Varshavski Dnevnik*, January 11, 1880, in *Sochineniya*, 7:74.

earthly paradise, lit by electric street-lights and talking by telephone from Kamchatka to the Cape of Good Hope."[30] A few months before his death Leontyev wrote to Rozanov that such inventions as the telephone and railroad were destroying

all organic life on earth—poetry, religion, the isolation of states and of everyday existence . . . , the "tree of knowledge" and the "tree of life." The intensification of movement is not in itself an intensification of life. The machine runs, but the living tree stands firm.[31]

Leontyev expressed the deadening effect of technology upon religion and the "poetry" of life in a miniature parable. In a remote Russian village a long black passenger train stands noisily at the grade crossing, completely blocking the peasants' religious procession. A passenger watches unconcernedly from a train window. The whole scene, for Leontyev, is simply "execrable."[32]

Leontyev was highly critical of what he called "anthropolatry"—the worship of secular man as man—but he identified anthropolatry, confusingly, with "individualism."[33] Thus he wrote that "individualism (individualizm) is destroying the individuality (individualnost) of human beings, of regions, and of nations."[34] To clear up such puzzles it will help to distinguish (although Leontyev himself failed explicitly to do so) between a "liberal-democratic," egalitarian, security-minded, self-enclosed

[30] Quoted in K. Medvedski, "Filosof-Khristianin: Osnovy mirosozertsaniya K. N. Leontyeva" [A Christian Philosopher: Fundamentals of K. N. Leontyev's World View], Russki Vestnik, 242 (January, 1896): 241.

[31] Letter to Rozanov, July 30, 1891, in Russki Vestnik, 285 (June, 1903):414.

[32] "Nashi novyie khristiane, II," in Sochineniya, 8:212.

[33] Nashi novyie khristiane: I: Strakh Bozhi i lyubov k chelovechestvu: Po povodu rasskaza L. N. Tolstovo 'Chem lyudi zhivy?' " [Our New Christians: I: Fear of God and Love of Mankind: On L. N. Tolstoy's Story "What Men Live By"] (1882), in Sochineniya, 8:160.

[34] "Vizantizm i Slavyanstvo," in Sochineniya, 5:147.

individualism on the one hand and a "conservative," hierarchical, risk-seeking, and creative individualism on the other. It is only the first kind—close to ordinary egoism—that Leontyev attacks. The second kind—which, if it is egoistic, represents the creative egoism of the artist—he plainly defends. (We may add that it was only the first kind of individualism that Herzen had attacked, contrasting the walled, selfish privacy of the French bourgeois to the unwalled openness of the Russians. Dostoyevski, similarly, had attacked the Europeans, especially the French, for their laissez-faire selfishness, expressed in the complacent rhetorical question "But am I my brother's keeper?")

Even in his early period of "aesthetic amoralism" Leontyev stopped short of glorifying the strong and creative individual in the way that Nietzsche later glorified the *freier Geist* and the *Übermensch*. After his religious conversion he ceased to celebrate individuality, doubtless feeling that to claim for mere man any autonomous creation of cultural, social, or moral values would be impious, involving the sin of intellectual and spiritual pride.

Like Nietzsche, Leontyev saw "contemporary European Christianity" as furthering the hated march of democratic and egalitarian "progress." In one place he went so far as to speak of the "anti-Christ" of democracy. Nietzsche, in contrast, considered *himself* the "anti-Christ" or "anti-Christian" (the German term *Antichrist* can mean either or both). Democratic egalitarianism for Nietzsche is "anti-anti-Christian," which, by negation of the negation, whether Aristotelian or Hegelian, makes it, if not "Christian," at least "pro-Christian." There is the further difference that Nietzsche recognized only one kind of Christianity, at least in nineteenth-century Europe, whereas Leontyev distinguished between the "pseudo-Christianity" of Western Europe and the "true Christianity" of Byzantium.

Nietzsche had made a punning distinction between Christian *Nächstenliebe* ("love of one's neighbor," literally "of the nearest") and Nietzschean anti-Christian *Fernstenliebe* ("love of the far-off," literally "of the farthest"). To love and help one's neighbor, according to Nietzsche, is to preserve the sick, the weak, the uncreative, and hence to impede or even cripple the vital culture of the future. Truly to love the far-off, the high culture created by a coming superhumanity (*Übermenschheit*)— for which the best representatives of the present generation serve only as a bridge—one must be cruel toward one's weak and suffering neighbor. Hence the hard Nietzschean saying: "When you see a man falling, kick him down!"

Leontyev's distinction, formulated several years before Nietzsche's, is couched in very similar terms. The Russian expressions are *lyubov k blizhnemu* ("love of one's neighbor," literally "of the nearest or closest") and *lyubov k dalnemu* ("love of the far-off"). But Leontyev reversed Nietzsche's value ascriptions; he rejected "love for the far-off" as "a feverish preoccupation with the earthly welfare of future generations" whose object is a "collective and abstract mankind."[35] In this rejection he was close to Herzen, who had branded the subordination of living individuals to future generations—"to society, to nation, humanity, or idea"—a "continuation of the practice of human sacrifice."[36]

In direct though of course unknowing opposition to Nietzsche, Leontyev defended the Christian concern for presently encountered, existing human beings: love "for the nearest, for the very nearest, the person met (*vstrechnomu*), the person at

[35] "Nashi novyie khristiane, II," in *Sochineniya*, 8:189, 207.
[36] Alexander Herzen, *From the Other Shore* (1850), ed. I. Berlin (London and New York, 1956), p. 134.

hand—a compassion for . . . the living and real human being whose tears we see, whose sighs and groans we hear, whose hand we can actually clasp, like a brother's, in *this present hour*."[37]

The contrast between Nietzsche and Leontyev, however, is not quite so sharp as the foregoing paragraphs may suggest. For one thing, although Nietzsche was indeed "feverishly preoccupied" with future generations, his concern was not for their "earthly welfare" but for their "cultural creativity," a very different sort of thing. Furthermore, Leontyev did not agree with those Christians, repudiated by Nietzsche, who held that compassion should be reserved, in Leontyev's words, for "suffering workers and wounded soldiers." Leontyev specifically insisted that true Christian compassion should include the strong, the beautiful, the high-placed: tsars, cardinals, popes, poets, and generals. It involved the "poetry" as well as the "prose" of social and historical life.[38]

Leontyev also is close to Nietzsche in his denial that it is either possible or desirable to make men secure against risk, contingency, and suffering. He charged European "pseudo-humanism" or "pseudo-humanitarianism"[39] with being sentimentally optimistic, blind to the "irremediable tragic character of life," deaf to the wisdom of Jeremiah and Ecclesiastes. Anthropolatrous pseudo-humanism, according to Leontyev, attempts to eliminate "those shocks, struggles, and sufferings

[37] "Nashi novyie khristiane, II," in *Sochineniya*, 8:207 (italics partially removed).

[38] In part, at least, because of such statements as this Berdyaev called Leontyev a "Nietzschean Christian," something *sui generis* (*Konstantin Leontyev*, p. 227).

[39] The Russian word, here translated as "humanism" or "humanitarianism," is *gumannost*; it could also be translated "humaneness."

which are useful to us"—not useful, of course, in any social-utilitarian sense but rather in a Christian-ascetic sense, as a discipline and tempering of the spirit.[40]

The European pseudo-humanists whom Leontyev had chiefly in mind were John Stuart Mill and his Russian followers: Chernyshevski, Dobrolyubov, and Pisarev—the "men of the sixties." All of them assumed, in Mill's words, that "most of the great positive evils of the world are in themselves removable" and that "all of the grand sources . . . of human suffering are in a great degree, many of them almost entirely, conquerable by human care and effort."[41]

The evils mentioned by Mill (and emphasized by Chernyshevski) are ignorance, poverty, disease, and the "vicissitudes of fortune." Neither Mill nor Chernyshevski ever mentioned the most radical evils of all: old age and death. It was precisely these evils that most concerned Leontyev, and he denied that they can be abolished by any collective social effort or by any conspiracy of silence. The contrary assumption is, for him, "consoling childishness" and complacent optimism. In 1890, reviewing Tolstoy's story *The Death of Ivan Ilyich*, Leontyev exclaimed:

In that bourgeois-commercial, spiritually desolate environment in which Ivan Ilyich moved (an environment, alas, all too familiar to us!) it is impossible to prepare men for death with Christian courage.[42]

Genuine Christian humanism or humaneness (*gumannost*) involves a "severe and sorrowful pessimism, a courageous submissiveness to the incorrigibility of earthly life."[43] In Leontyev's

[40] "Nashi novyie khristiane, II," in *Sochineniya*, 8: 203 (italics removed).

[41] J. S. Mill, *Utilitarianism* (1863), in E. A. Burtt, ed., *The English Philosophers from Bacon to Mill* (New York, 1939), pp. 906, 907.

[42] Analiz, stil i veyaniye: o romanakh gr. L. N. Tolstovo," in *Sochineniya*, 8:271 (italics removed); Brown University Reprint, p. 55.

[43] "Nashi novyie khristiane, II," in *Sochineniya*, 8:189.

view, both Dostoyevski and Tolstoy were insensitive to this "incorrigibility," blind to the "deeply disturbing, eternal tragedy of history." (Berdyaev argues plausibly that this charge applies to Tolstoy but not to Dostoyevski.) [44]

Leontyev distinguished, perhaps not sharply enough, between the "true" Christianity of Dostoyevski's novels—especially *Crime and Punishment, The Possessed,* and *The Brothers Karamazov*—and the "pseudo-Christianity" of his Pushkin Day address of 1880. It is the latter which, with some justice, Leontyev assimilates to Tolstoy's position.

Leontyev attacked Tolstoy's reduction of religion to ethics and the "law of love." As Rozanov pointed out, Leontyev had the temerity to repudiate Christian meekness (*krotost*), considering it a doubtful "virtue" that furthered the spirit of *meshchanstvo*, Philistinism. [45] This too was a point of intellectual contact with Nietzsche. Leontyev regarded Tolstoy's religious position as "saccharine, sentimental, rose-colored, and utilitarian-moral" rather than "mystical-dogmatic." [46] He charged, further, that it played into the hands of the European pseudo-humanists.

Religion that is only love of man, Leontyev insists, verges on pseudo-Christianity and anthropolatry; true Christianity is based not so much on love of man as on fear of God. "One must live to that point," Leontyev once wrote, "grow to that point where one genuinely fears God, with a simple, almost animal, fear . . . , a plain terror of sinning." [47] He added that fear of the Lord is the beginning and root of wisdom and love is only its fruit. "One

[44] *Konstantin Leontyev,* p. 232.

[45] "Neuznanny fenomen," p. 156.

[46] Letter to Rozanov, August 13, 1891, in *Russki Vestnik,* 285 (June, 1903): 416.

[47] Letter to A. A. Aleksandrov, July 24, 1887, in *Bogoslovski Vestnik,* no. 3 (1914), pp. 458 f.

must not mistake the fruit for its root, or the root for its fruit."[48]

Bulgakov, who has paid more attention than most commentators to the theme of the "fear of God" in Leontyev's final religious position, quoted Leontyev's somber statement about the "red icon-lamp" at the Optina Pustyn monastery that sometimes seemed "unbearably terrifying, in the dark, among the snows." This, Bulgakov comments, is the *terror antiquus*. He adds that although some of Leontyev's early stories expressed the joy of life, when Leontyev turned to religion "everything became dark, black shadows fell across the earth, fear settled upon his soul. *Timor fecit deos*, or more precisely, *religionem*." In Leontyev's religion, Bulgakov concludes, a religion "born in terror and supported by an effort of will, there was always something strained (*nadryvny*)."[49]

As we have seen, Leontyev admitted to a concern for "personal salvation"; he used the expression 'transcendental egoism' to characterize his own religious position. In a lyrical passage he expressed his final desire: "Beneath the ringing of the monastery bells, unceasingly reminding us of the eternity which is now so close, to become indifferent to everything in the world except my own soul and the concern for its purification."[50]

Earlier Leontyev had taken aesthetic delight in the sonorous and plastic beauty of the Russian Orthodox service. In the monastery at Mt. Athos (in 1870 and 1871) he managed to preserve the "aesthetics of life," or at least an active interest in secular culture. "Side by side, on my desk," he wrote, "are Proudhon and the Prophet David; Byron and St. John Chrysostom;

---

[48] "Nashi novyie khristiane, I," in *Sochineniya*, 8:159, 183.
[49] "Pobeditel-Pobezhdyonny," in *Tikhiye dumy*, pp. 115, 116, 127.
[50] Quoted in Berdyaev, *Konstantin Leontyev*, p. 224.

John of Damascus and Goethe; Khomyakov and Herzen. . . . Here I love the world as though it were a distant and harmless tableau."[51]

In his last years, however, Leontyev came to feel with increasing sharpness the conflict between his Byzantine Orthodoxy and his treasured "aesthetics of life." For the individual, he declared, Byzantine Orthodoxy is "a religion of disillusionment, a religion without hope for anything earthly."[52] And thus, of course, without hope for culture, beauty, or the "aesthetics of life."

From the Optina Pustyn monastery Leontyev wrote to Rozanov: "Christian preaching and European progress are joining forces to kill the aesthetics of life on earth. . . . What are we to do? We must assist Christianity even to the detriment of our beloved aesthetics."[53] In an earlier letter he had said flatly: "Only the poetry of religion can erode the poetry of exquisite immorality."[54]

The religious position which Leontyev adopted in his last years has a marked Old Testament—as opposed to New Testament—coloring, probably at least in part as a result of the Islamic influences to which he had earlier been exposed. In Bulgakov's phrase, Leontyev's "Christianity" is shrouded in the

[51] "Chetyre pisma s Afona" [Four Letters from Mt. Athos], *Bogoslovski Vestnik*, no. 11 (1912), p. 464 (italics removed). This is a semi-fictional, semi-autobiographical work in epistolary form, written in 1884. The "letter" here quoted is dated June 1, 1872.

[52] "Chetyre pisma" (letter dated July 23, 1872), *Bogoslovski Vestnik*, no. 12 (1912), p. 707. Solovyov had pointed out a contradiction between Leontyev's mystical claim that everything earthly is only a "swiftly passing dream" and his historical ideal of a complex and flourishing "neo-Byzantine culture." As Solovyov drily notes, if history as a whole is only a passing dream, so is neo-Byzantine culture ("Pamyati K. N. Leontyeva," p. 357).

[53] Quoted in Berdyaev, *Konstantin Leontyev*, p. 249.

[54] Letter to A. A. Aleksandrov, July 24, 1887, *Bogoslovski Vestnik*, no. 3 (1914), p. 456.

"sackcloth and ashes" not of the Old Testament but of Islam.[55] Berdyaev adds that Leontyev placed much greater stress on God the Father—transcendent, wrathful, and punishing—than on the Son—immanent, compassionate, and redemptive.[56] He failed to develop even the outlines of a doctrine of "Godman-hood" (*Bogochelovechestvo*), a theme that had been central for Solovyov and was to be central for Bulgakov, Frank, and Berdyaev.

II

Leontyev deliberately shifted the accent away from the Gospel Christianity of sacrificial love and forgiveness—from "Jesus meek and mild"—to the wrathful Jehovah who judges and punishes. Rozanov continued the de-emphasis of the New Testament, but what he found in the Old Testament was not so much a judge as a *father*, in the sense of a giver-of-life and founder of families. Rozanov's God has more than a touch of the Homeric Zeus, *pater andrōn te theōn te* ("father of men and gods"). In combining pagan and Christian motifs Rozanov was very much in the spirit of the Russian "new religious consciousness" of the early twentieth century, whose spokesmen—especially Merezhkovski—liked to invoke "the suffering Christ and the great god Pan."

Vasili Vasilyevich Rozanov was born in 1856 (twenty-five years after Leontyev) into a poor provincial family. His grandfather was a village priest of the non-celibate Russian Orthodox "white clergy." His widowed mother, overworked and distraught, gave him little affection. He tells us that his first reaction to his

---

[55] "Pobeditel-Pobezhdyonny," in *Tikhiye dumy*, p. 127.
[56] *Konstantin Leontyev*, p. 226.

mother's death was relief that at last he could smoke openly (he was then thirteen)![57]

Rozanov attended *gymnasia* at Kostroma, Simbirsk, and Nizhni Novgorod, and then Moscow University, studying history and literature, but not very attentively. He later boasted of having "slept through" all of his courses at the university, although he also admitted that it was there he had acquired his love for philosophy. Upon graduation he became a teacher of history and geography in provincial schools. His first book, a long and ponderous philosophical treatise, appeared in 1886—when he was thirty—but, like Hume's *Treatise*, it fell "stillborn" from the press. During this period Rozanov also translated works of Aristotle into Russian.

Rozanov greatly admired Dostoyevski, and his first major work was a philosophical and critical study called *The Legend of the Grand Inquisitor* (1891). In 1880, when he was twenty-four years old and still at Moscow University, he had married Dostoyevski's former mistress, the forty-year-old Apollinaria Suslova. One of his motives was a desire to establish a personal link with his literary hero, whom he had never met. In fact, Dostoyevski died the following year, and Rozanov did not meet him. Suslova made Rozanov's life as miserable as she had made Dostoyevski's; she left him after six stormy years but refused to grant him a divorce, which after 1889 he very much wanted in order to marry a young widow named Barbara Rudneva. From 1891, when he married Rudneva in a secret church ceremony with the blessing of the local clergy, until 1918, when Suslova died, Rozanov was technically a bigamist and his five children by Rudneva were technically illegitimate (he had to "adopt"

[57] V. V. Rozanov, *Solitaria*, "with an Abridged Account of the Author's Life . . . and Matter from *The Apocalypse of Our Times*," trans. S. S. Koteliansky (London and New York, 1927), p. 130.

them). This "bigamous" marriage, however, was a happy one; Rozanov was devoted to his wife and often referred to her in his later writings with deep affection.

After twelve years of not very successful teaching in the provinces, during which he published many articles and later collected a number of them into books, Rozanov took a government position in St. Petersburg in 1893, which he held until 1899. Once established in the capital, he rapidly became a professional writer, both for the conservative *Novoye Vremya* and, under the pseudonym "Varvarin,"[58] for the radical *Russkoye Slovo*.[59]

Rozanov's early works, such as *Semeiny vopros v Rossii* [The Family Question in Russia] (2 vols. 1903) and *Okolo tserkovnykh sten* [By the Walls of the Church] (2 vols. 1906) were unusual in that as much as a quarter or even a third of their text was made up of letters which Rozanov had received from provincial teachers, village priests, St. Petersburg atheists, retired generals, and the like, with Rozanov's detailed commentaries.

His later works, published after 1911—especially *Solitaria, Fallen Leaves* (two vols.), and *The Apocalypse of Our Time*— are written in a fragmented, aphoristic style that is reminiscent of Nietzsche—with one significant exception. Apart from an occasional preface dated in the Swiss or Italian Alps, Nietzsche does not give his readers any indication of the circumstances under which a given fragment or aphorism was composed.

[58] Rozanov disliked his family name. The pseudonym he chose combines a reference to his wife, whose given name in Russian is Varvara, and the adjective 'barbarian' (*varvarski*).

[59] Rozanov confessed that at one point he was writing politically conservative and politically radical articles with equal conviction (*Opavshiye listya* [Fallen Leaves] (1913), 1:159–61). One critic suggests that he did this, at least in part, to discredit fashionable ideological pigeonholes and to turn his readers' attention to matters that he considered much more important (Joseph Czapski in the preface to Vassily Rozanov's *La Face sombre du Christ*, trans. Nathalie Reznikoff [Paris, 1964], p. 25).

Rozanov, in both *Solitaria* and *Fallen Leaves*, regularly identified his aphorisms as having been written "over morning coffee," "at afternoon tea," "while looking at my coin collection," "on getting up early in the morning," "on the train," and the like, often with the exact date. Some of these notes throw revealing light on the aphorisms; for example, "I do not want truth, I want peace"—written "after the doctor's visit."[60]

Rozanov was often castigated, and with good reason, for his lack of principle. He defended some of the most reactionary tsarist policies and he approved Tolstoy's excommunication in 1901, although he criticized the Holy Synod for its impersonal and bureaucratic handling of the affair. It would have been more appropriate, Rozanov suggested, for Tolstoy to have been "driven out of the Church" by a band of the outraged peasants whose religious sensibilities he had offended. Rozanov even lent his support, on occasion, to official anti-Semitism, despite the fact that in his religious views he was very close to the Old Testament. The St. Petersburg Religious and Philosophical Society, an organization that provided a unique point of contact between secular intellectuals and the Russian Orthodox clergy, formally expelled him in 1913 for his anti-Semitic writings.

The months after October, 1917, were marked by great hardship and suffering for Rozanov. Close to actual starvation, he once walked to Moscow in severe winter cold from the Trinity Monastery of St. Sergius in Sergiyev Posad (now called Zagorsk), where he was then living—a distance of almost forty miles—in

[60] *Opavshiye listya*, 1:381; *Izbrannoye*, p. 286; *Fallen Leaves*, p. 120. (Only the first volume of *Opavshiye listya* [Fallen Leaves] has been translated into English, but brief excerpts from both volumes are included in *Izbrannoye*, selections of Rozanov's writings that were published in New York in 1956, ed. by Yuri Ivask. Because the original volumes, as well as the translation, have long been out of print, references will be given, where appropriate, to *Izbrannoye*).

search of food. He died in January, 1919, and was buried, following his request, beside Leontyev in the cemetery of the monastery at Sergiyev Posad.[61]

Despite his close and happy family life, Rozanov was in many ways a lonely man, rather like Leontyev in his final years. In the late Rozanov, as in Kierkegaard, the "objective world" tends to recede into the background, although in the works of his middle period there is a definite cosmological accent. Rozanov himself once said: "I am . . . all subject; the subjective is really developed in me to an infinite degree, to a degree that I . . . do not suspect in anyone else."[62]

One of Rozanov's first critics called his books "simply a chaotic diary . . .—the diary of a great soul which does not itself know what it contains and what is important in it." The same critic, however, went on to say that, in these "autobiographical" and journal-like books, Rozanov seldom speaks about his own writing or his encounters with editors, publishers, or other writers—the autobiographical remarks being mostly affectionate references to his family, to the civil service, to the cities and villages he has visited, and the like.[63]

What Rozanov said of Leontyev as a thinker applies in his own case: he had neither teachers nor disciples; he came from no school and founded none. In fact, Rozanov strikes one as a more independent and original—though not necessarily more profound—thinker than either his older contemporary Leontyev or his younger contemporary Shestov. The immediacy, bril-

[61] See M. Kurdyumov, O Rozanove [On Rozanov] (Paris, 1929), pp. 84 f.

[62] Uyedinyonnoye [Solitude] (St. Petersburg, 1912), p. 56; Izbrannoye, p. 204; Solitaria, p. 67.

[63] B. Griftsov, Tri myslitelya: V. Rozanov, D. Merezhkovski, L. Shestov [Three Thinkers: V. Rozanov, D. Merezhkovski, L. Shestov] (Moscow, 1911), pp. 19, 80.

liance, and "Russianness" of his style have been attested by such expert witnesses as the philosopher Berdyaev, the critic Mirsky, and the writer Remizov.

Rozanov was no less impatient than Leontyev had been with Tolstoy's moralizing but he took Tolstoy seriously as a religious thinker and acknowledged that Tolstoy had experienced much anguish, indeed, "the sufferings of Job." Tolstoy, he says, constructed his works carefully—with ruler, plumbline, and hammer, eyeing a blueprint. As a result, he astonishes and "convinces" us, but does not move us (as Dostoyevski does).[64] In 1902 Rozanov wrote that Tolstoy, "despite his dreadful . . . mistakes and sharp words, is an enormous religious phenomenon, perhaps the greatest phenomenon—though a distorted one —in Russian religious history of the nineteenth century."[65]

One of the "mistakes and distortions" that Rozanov detected in Tolstoy was the Schopenhauerian Buddhism, or quasi-Buddhism, that we examined in chapter 1. Rozanov criticized this position with explicit reference not to Tolstoy himself but to his associate and disciple, N. N. Strakhov. Rozanov considered Buddha an "atheistic sage" who lacked faith.

With faith—it is joyful; with faith it is good; with faith "I love" and "we love"; with faith apples grow, and cherries blossom; where there is faith—the maidens dance. But what waltz will you dance in nirvana?[66]

According to Rozanov, Buddha, like Schopenhauer (and, we may add, Tolstoy), was moved mainly by fear of death. Death

[64] *Opavshiye listya*, 2.:219 and *Izbrannoye*, p. 343.

[65] *Okolo tserkovnykh sten* [By the Walls of the Church] (St. Petersburg, 1906), 2:452.

[66] From Rozanov's commentary on Strakhov's letter to him, dated January 22, 1893, in *Literaturnyie izgnanniki* [Literary Exiles], 1:345 n., and *Izbrannoye*, pp. 186 f.

is black and terrible, Rozanov argued, only because life is radiant and joyful: "The end is dreadful because the path is splendid." To make the end of life less dreadful, Buddha was ready to extinguish the radiance of life's path. Buddhism "vanquishes" death, but only at the cost of stifling and deadening life. Nirvana, a state like that of primordial chaos "before the creation of the world," cannot replace

the single lovely smile, with which a young girl goes into the morning garden, picks fresh roses, takes them back to her room, puts them in a glass of water, and stands admiring them. To be sure, the roses will wither, the glass will be broken, and the girl will die. But why should I concentrate my thoughts on that morning, and that "very hour," when "in thirty years" the girl will die, and the glass will be broken, rather than on the glass and the roses and the girl and her smile as they are now?[67]

This is a clear antithesis to the Buddhism of Tolstoy's last years (we recall Halley's Comet). It conveys a sense, which Rozanov elsewhere makes explicit, of joy in living and gratitude for the gift of life—very different from Tolstoy's bleak moralism though very close to the feeling expressed by Pasternak in Dr. Zhivago and in his later religious poetry. Rozanov said that he wrote Solitaria "to give thanks for every moment of existence and to make every moment of existence eternal."[68]

Rozanov disliked moralizing of every kind—not just the humorless religious asceticism of Tolstoy and the Tolstoyans but also the humorless revolutionary asceticism of the socialists. In an early aphorism he gently deflated the latter's earnest commitment to socio-political action. " 'What's to be done?'[69]

[67] Literaturnyie izgnanniki, 1:346 n., and Izbrannoye, pp. 187 f.

[68] Opavshiye listya, 2:437, and Izbrannoye, p. 377.

[69] In Russian, "Chto delat?" This also is the title of a well-known revolutionary novel by Chernyshevski (1863), and Lenin used it as the title for an equally well-known revolutionary pamphlet (1902).

demanded an impatient young man of Petersburg. 'Well, here is what's to be done: If it is *summertime*, pick over the berries and make the jam; if it is *winter*—drink your tea, sweetened with the jam.' "[70]

Rozanov shows his contempt for moralizing, and for morality of a conventional kind, by refusing to take it seriously. "I am not an enemy of morality," he declared; "it simply never enters my mind." And again: "I am not yet such a scoundrel as to think of morality; . . . I don't even know whether it is spelled with one *l* or two."[71]

Rozanov made a similar wry comment about duty. He had always lived, he says, "by taste, by what I wanted and what I liked," and the idea of duty never occurred to him. "I only read about it in the dictionary under the letter *D*."

Rozanov's conclusion is wholly in the spirit of Nietzsche's Zarathustra: " 'Duty was invented by cruel men to oppress the weak. And only fools obey it.' Something like that. . . ."[72] This position might be called an "amoralism," although Rozanov himself seldom used the term. It is quite different, however, from Leontyev's aesthetic amoralism or Nietzsche's cultural amoralism. Rozanov subordinated morality neither to the "aesthetics of life," with Leontyev, nor to the "aesthetics of (future) culture," with Nietzsche, but to the unique and non-recurrent existence of living individuals. In this "existential" emphasis he was perhaps inspired most directly by Dostoyevski.

Rozanov expressed both the precariousness and the precious-

---

[70] "Embriony" [Embryos] (1899), in *Religiya i kultura*, 2d. ed. (St. Petersburg, 1901), p. 239, and *Izbrannoye*, p. 63.

[71] *Uyedinyonnoye*, pp. 152, 155; *Solitaria*, p. 98. What the translator renders in English as the difference between "one *l* and two" is the rather subtler difference in Russian between two forms of the letter *e* in the spelling of *nravstvennost*.

[72] *Ibid.*, pp. 184 f.; *Solitaria*, p. 108.

ness of individual existence in a metaphor that combines the two Greek meanings of *psychē*, "soul" and "butterfly." (The butterfly lives but a day after it emerges from the chrysalis, and its brief life is purely "sexual." It does not eat—in some species it lacks even digestive organs; it merely procreates.) Rozanov's present purpose is to explain his rejection of the constraints of moral norms and prohibitions:

A million years went by before my soul was let out into the world to delight in it; how can I suddenly say to her: Don't let yourself go, my pet, enjoy yourself only in a moral fashion. No, I say to her: Enjoy yourself, my pet, have a good time, my precious, enjoy yourself in any way you please. And toward evening you will go to God. For my life is my day, and it is *my day*, not that of Socrates or Spinoza.[73]

Rozanov's approach to morality and (as we shall see) to religion as well was highly personal and individual. It was not in the least "world-historical" or future-oriented—in Nietzsche's sense of "subordinated to a future historical culture." For Rozanov, every individual existence has intrinsic value.[74] For Nietzsche, no individual has intrinsic value; individuals have instrumental value only as creators and "transvaluators" of values, whose creativity serves future history, enriching the cumulative culture that is in process of becoming. One way to put the difference is to say that Nietzsche is a post-Hegelian

---

[73] *Ibid.*, p. 152; *Solitaria*, p. 98.
[74] One commentator has noted that Rozanov adpoted Dostoyevski's principle of the absolute value (and freedom) of the individual person (Paolo Leskovec, S.J., *Basilio Rozanov e la sua concezione religiosa*, Orientalia Christiana Analecta no. 151 [Rome, 1958], p. 25). Rozanov himself declared in 1892: "A man does not want to be only a means" (*Literaturnyie ocherki* [St. Petersburg, 1899], p. 106). In contrast, in Nietzsche's view, all men are means or instruments—positive or negative, creative, passive, or obstructive—for achieving a higher culture.

thinker whereas Rozanov, like Kant and Kierkegaard, is a "pre-Hegelian" or, at least, anti-Hegelian thinker. But, of course, although Nietzsche's stress on culture and history is in a broad sense Hegelian, his stress on *future* culture and history is quite un-Hegelian. (We shall return to this question in chapter 4.)

Rozanov shared Nietzsche's—and Leontyev's—contempt for European humanism or humanitarianism (*gumannost*), calling it an "icy love." "Pseudo-compassion" (*lzhe-sostradatelnost*) he insisted, was ruining European civilization.[75] Rozanov also opposed the reigning liberalism and what he called "wooden, nonsensical positivism."[76] He was almost as critical of technology as Leontyev had been. And science and scholarship[77] constituted a "new despot" that held truth in its claws and smothered it with jargon.

In contrast to all of this, religion stands for joy and freedom. And by "religion" Rozanov means primarily Russian Orthodoxy. After a visit to Rome in 1909 he wrote sympathetically and admiringly of Roman Catholicism; but he had little use for Protestantism. The Protestant service, conducted in an "emptied" church—"emptied," that is, of icons, candles, and ornate altars—was nothing but "a lecture plus a concert."[78]

Christianity, Rozanov had written in 1899, "is joy, only joy, and joy always." It is "the sweat, pain, and joy of a mother giving birth, the cry of a new-born babe."[79] In its joy of life Christianity is closer to Epicureanism than to Stoicism, which is redo-

[75] *Opavshiye listya*, 1:370; *Izbrannoye*, pp. 284, 285; *Fallen Leaves*, p. 116.

[76] *Opavshiye listya*, 1:490; *Izbrannoye*, p. 300; *Fallen Leaves*, p. 152.

[77] As we have seen, the Russian term *nauka*, like the German *Wissenschaft*, includes scholarship as well as science.

[78] "Embriony," in *Religiya i kultura*, p. 245, and *Izbrannoye*, pp. 68 f.

[79] "Embriony," in *Religiya i kultura*, pp. 243 f., and *Izbrannoye*, p. 67.

lent of death." Christianity does not stress man's sinfulness: since Christ has saved men, "our only sin . . . is to assume that we are still sinful, not holy. We are holy: this is the true ecstasy (*vostorg*) of the Christian; we are free . . . not with an outer independence, but with an inner freedom from sin."[80]

Even in Rozanov's early works (up to 1906), however, there is more than a hint of dissatisfaction with Christianity. In 1899 he called the Gospels "an absolutization of chastity"[81] and he contrasted "fleshly antiquity" (*plotskaya drevnost*) with "castrated contemporaneity" (*skopcheskaya sovremennost*). Contemporary religion, he said, demands sacred groves and maidens holding hands as they dance in a circle.

As early as 1899 Rozanov pointed out that in the Old Testament there is almost no conception of sin, adding that the task of the twentieth century will be to resurrect the "flesh and blood of the Old Testament."[82] This "resurrection" was carried out in his two-volume work of 1906, *Okolo tserkovnykh sten* [By the Walls of the Church], in which he made the Kierkegaardian point (although he did not mention Kierkegaard and probably had not read him) that the Incarnation— the suffering and death in time of a deathless and eternal being —is a shock to all ancient religious conceptions and a "destruction" of the Old Testament.[83] He goes on to contrast the Old and New Testaments:

In the Old people love, give birth, fall in love . . . ; in the New

[80] *Okolo tserkovnykh sten*, 1:19.

[81] "Khristianstvo passivno ili aktivno?" [Passive or Active Christianity?] in *Religiya i kultura*, p. 156.

[82] Polemicheskiye materialy" [Polemical Materials] (1899), in *V mire neyasnovo i nereshyonnovo* [In the World of the Uncertain and Obscure] (St. Petersburg, 1901), p. 193, n. 1.

[83] *Okolo tserkovnykh sten*, 2:482. Rozanov's expression is "*razrusheniye Biblii*," literally "destruction of the Bible." In Russian *Bibliya* is used for the Old Testament, *Yevangeliye* for the New Testament.

they do not give birth and in this sense do not love . . . ; in the New Testament there is no smile; no one is depicted as smiling.[84]

Later, Rozanov commented that "what is most apocalyptic in us is our smile."[85]

The New Testament, Rozanov continues, says nothing about smells; there is nothing aromatic in it, "as if to emphasize its divergence from the flower of the Bible, the Song of Songs." The New Testament lacks the power and passion of the Old. It contains "no songs, no joys, no ecstasies, no looking up to Heaven"—no King David singing psalms of praise.[86]

More generally, according to Rozanov, "The New Testament is related to the Old as death to conception, as burial to birth, as the monastery to the family. . . ."[87] Rozanov saw the monastery as essential to Christianity, "the seed from which all of Christianity, as a historical phenomenon, has grown." And he adds: "Just as the grave is a transformation of death 'into poetry,' so the monastery is a transformation of 'the grave' into an entire civilization."[88] Christianity, he said in 1909, is a "funereal culture."[89] Earlier he had called the Christian church a "worship of the grave . . . , of Christ in His grave. . . . Nothing about the existence of Christ has been made into such a great and constant symbol as His death."[90]

---

[84] Ibid., p. 477.

[85] The Apocalypse of Our Times, trans. James M. Edie and James P. Scanlan, in Russian Philosophy, 2:297.

[86] Ibid., pp. 297 f.

[87] Okolo tserkovnykh sten, 2:481. Rozanov makes a punning distinction (which cannot be reproduced in English) between the book of Genesis, which in Russian is called Kniga Bytiya (literally "The Book of Being or Existence"), and nebytiyo (the "non-being" or "death") of the New Testament.

[88] Ibid., p. 480.

[89] Italyanskiye vpechatleniya [Italian impressions] (St. Petersburg, 1909), p. 121.

[90] Okolo tserkovnykh sten, 2:445.

With specific reference to Russian Christianity, Rozanov adds:

. . . Russia finds the earthly life of the Saviour too real and coarse; she listens with only half an ear to His teaching, His parables and sermons. . . . But as soon as the Saviour comes close to the cross Russia pricks up her ears, heart pounding. Christ has died—Russia is overwhelmed with consternation.[91]

The death cult of Golgotha, Rozanov feels, has overshadowed the life cult of Bethlehem. He likes to picture the "God-man" in the cradle surrounded by oxen and beneath the star—an image strikingly developed in the poem "Star of the Nativity" in Pasternak's Zhivago cycle. "How brief is the rite of baptism, how dull the ceremony of wedding, how hasty the sacrament of confession and communion: But a man dies, and Christianity rises in all its power: what songs, what words, what thoughts, what poetry!" Earlier Rozanov had complained that "no one venerates a new-born baby; [but] everyone venerates the dead."[92]

The Gospel, for Rozanov, is essentially not the "good news" of resurrection and life everlasting but the gloomy tidings of the death of God. And Christ "did not plant a single tree, did not engender the smallest plant. . . ."[93]

In an article of 1907, "Sweetest Jesus and the Bitter Fruits of the World," Rozanov set forth in detail his identification of Christ with death and the denial of procreation and life. Berdyaev found the article "fascinating" and brilliantly written, but fundamentally mistaken. According to Rozanov, Berdyaev wrote, "the world has grown bitter in Christ. Those who have loved Christ have lost their taste for the world. . . . The family, science and scholarship, art, the joy of earthly life—all are either

[91] Russkaya tserkov [The Russian Church] (St. Petersburg, 1909), p. 5.
[92] Semeiny vopros v Rossii [The Family Question in Russia] (St. Petersburg, 1903), 2:9.
[93] The Apocalypse of Our Times, in Russian Philosophy, 2:290.

bitter or without taste for one who has known the heavenly sweetness of Jesus." Christ, in Rozanov's view, taught men "not to love existence, [but] to love non-existence."[94]

Berdyaev's critique is two-pronged. On the one hand he accuses Rozanov of equating existence (*bytiyo*) with "everyday life (*byt*)" and of falling back on a pagan or Judaic "immanent sense of life" or "immanentist pantheism" that ignores Christian transcendence. If Rozanov took the doctrine of the *Resurrection* seriously, Berdyaev said, he could not have characterized Christianity as a "religion of death." On the other hand he accused Rozanov of overstating the ascetic and life-denying side of Christianity, pointing out that in its time Christianity had defended the "flesh of the world . . . against the spiritualistic denials of Platonism, gnosticism, etc."[95]

Rozanov suggests that the religion of "God-the-Father," which is historically related to sun worship, must replace the religion of "God-the-Son," which is a kind of moon worship, reflecting the "dark face" of Christianity—a religion not of life but of death.[96] In his later works Rozanov even referred to the "evil of Christ's coming," declaring that "Christ has intolerably burdened human life," casting "a mysterious shadow that has withered all grains." "The whole act of atonement has evaded man and thundered into an abyss, a wasteland, without saving anyone or anything."[97]

[94] "Khristos i mir: Otvet V. V. Rozanovu" [Christ and the World: An Answer to V. V. Rozanov] (1908), in *Dukhovny krizis intelligentsii: Stati po obshchestvennoi i religioznoi psikhologii* [The Spiritual Crisis of the Intelligentsia: Articles on Social and Religious psychology] (St. Petersburg, 1910), pp. 235, 236.

[95] *Ibid.*, p. 242 n.

[96] The Russian words for "son" (*syn*) and "sun" (*solntse*) are quite distinct.

[97] Quoted in V. V. Zenkovsky, *A History of Russian Philosophy*, trans. George L. Kline (London: Routledge & Kegan Paul; New York: Columbia University Press, 1953), 1:462, 457.

In *The Apocalypse of Our Time* Rozanov quoted with disapproval the saying of Jesus: "There are eunuchs who have made themselves eunuchs for the sake of the Kingdom of Heaven" (Matt. 19:12).[98] The New Testament, in Rozanov's view, accepts marriage and the family only grudgingly. Everything connected with procreation is considered sinful and filthy. The sexual realm is identified with the realm of Satan. Indeed, the extremist Russian sect of *skoptsy* (*castrati*) is only a *reductio ad absurdum* of the whole drift of the New Testament.

When Rozanov discussed marriage and the family with the aging and ascetic Tolstoy he found the same attitude. Tolstoy was "muddled . . . like a schoolboy who is not sure of his spelling; . . . essentially, he had nothing to say . . . except: 'One must abstain.' No analysis, . . . no *thought*; mere exclamations. One can't react to that, it is something *imbécile*."[99]

Rozanov did not hesitate to identify cosmic creativity with biological generation: "The connection of sex with God," he writes, "greater than the connection of mind with God, greater even than the connection of conscience with God, is evident from the fact that all a-sexual men reveal themselves as a-theists."[100] As early as 1899 Rozanov had declared that "where there is no sense of sex there is no sense of God,"[101] adding that the way to block the secularization and "castration" of contemporary civilization was to "pour religion into sex itself."[102] In 1903 he called the "unblemished family" a "tiny church" (*malenkaya tserkovka*). Ten years later, at a meeting of the Petersburg Religious and Philosophical Society, he made a

[98] *The Apocalypse of Our Times*, in *Russian Philosophy*, 2:294.
[99] *Uyedinyonnoye*, p. 231; *Solitaria*, p. 122.
[100] *Ibid.*, p. 169; *Solitaria*, p. 103.
[101] "Iz zagadok chelovecheskoi prirody" [From the Enigmas of Human Nature] (1898 or 1899), in *V mire neyasnovo*, p. 18.
[102] *Religiya i kultura*, p. 197.

proposal that shocked both clergymen and secular intellectuals: that newlyweds live for two or three months in the church where they had been married—until the woman was pregnant. The couples would sleep in small "bridal chambers," provided with icons and candles, close to flowering gardens and open to the stars. Their union would thus be "*in nature* and at the same time *in the temple*."[103]

It must be emphasized that Rozanov was neither a romantic nor a voluptuary.[104] Like D. H. Lawrence, he glorified not sensual pleasure but sexual creativity. The union of man and woman, the birth of a child, were for him mystical and sacred events. "From every humble cottage," Rozanov once wrote, "at the birth of every new self, our earth emits a tiny ray, and the whole earth glows. . . . The earth, when it gives birth, . . . becomes religiously radiant."[105] At the turn of the century Rozanov had referred to "dirty diapers and a naked wife" as the "truth of Bethlehem" around us.[106]

Berdyaev, on this point a somewhat cranky romantic, wanted to distinguish between personal love, on the one hand, and procreation and family life on the other. The latter, he asserts, often destroys the former. The family is "this world, a closing

[103] *Opavshiye listya*, 1:61; *Izbrannoye*, p. 244; *Fallen Leaves*, p. 17.

[104] Fr. Leskovec seems quite mistaken when he calls Rozanov's position a "naturalistic phallic mysticism" (*Basilio Rozanov*, p. 195); Ivanov-Razumnik is rather closer to the mark in speaking of Rozanov's "sexual gnosticism" (*Tvorchestvo i kritika* [Creativity and Criticism] [1922], p. 156).

[105] Quoted in Zenkovsky, *History of Russian Philosophy*, 1:459.

[106] "Brak i khristianstvo" [Marriage and Christianity] (1898), in *V mire neyasnovo*, p. 109. An Orthodox critic denies that Rozanov's is a "religion of Bethlehem." The true sacrament of Bethlehem, he asserts, "is not a pastoral scene of family tenderness, as Rozanov would have it, but the flaming mystery of the Incarnation. It is not the joy of human birth so much as the glory of the Divine descent [*niskhozhdeniye*]." (G. Florovsky, *Puti russkovo bogosloviya* [The Paths of Russian Theology], [Paris, 1937], p. 460).

in of horizons"; romantic love is "the other world, an opening up of horizons to infinity."[107] The family represents "immanence"; love as eros represents "transcendence." "This world" is chaotic, dead, "slavish"; birth is the "principle or beginning (nachalo) of death." "The perfected individual neither engenders nor dies."[108] Rozanov proposes, with his metaphysics of sex and family life, "to console us with the fecundity of decaying corpses."[109]

Rozanov was deterred neither by the romanticism nor the tastelessness of his critic; he continued, to the end, to stress the sanctity of family life. In the Old Testament, he declared, the Father "takes his child in his arms: He bathes it and cleans it and wipes its wet bottom."[110]

Berdyaev protested that Rozanov, with his stress on procreation and the "earthly Aphrodite," was close to Tolstoy, attempting to vanquish death by waving a green-and-yellow-spotted diaper. But child-bearing and child-rearing, Berdyaev insists, "save" the species, not the individual. The individual can be saved only by the transcendence of the "heavenly Aphrodite."[111]

Rozanov was unimpressed; he continued to glorify family life *tout court*, just as it is, without the idealization of the early Tolstoy. He announced the "stupendous truth" that

private life is above everything else. . . . Just sitting at home, and even picking your nose, and looking at the sunset . . . this is more universal than religion. . . . All religions will pass, but this will remain: simply sitting in a chair and looking into the distance.[112]

[107] "Khristos i mir," in *Dukhovny krizis intelligentsii*, p. 242.

[108] "Metafizika pola i lyubvi" [The Metaphysics of Sex and Love], in *Novoye religioznoye soznaniye i obshchestvennost* [The New Religious Consciousness and Society] (1907), pp. 163 f.

[109] "Khristos i mir," in *Dukhovny krizis intelligentsii*, p. 245.

[110] The Apocalypse of Our Times, in *Russian Philosophy*, 2:294.

[111] "Khristos i mir," in *Dukhovny krizis intelligentsii*, pp. 240, 241.

[112] *Uyedinyonnoye*, p. 145, and *Solitaria*, p. 96.

Rosanov refused to admit the triviality of domestic *trivia*. Each detail is sacred: "I want to arrive in the other world," he wrote, "with the handkerchief with which I blow my nose. Not a bit less." It was such statements as this that prompted Berdyaev to call Rozanov a *genialny obyvatel*, a "Philistine of genius."[113]

In other places Rozanov expanded the "warm round home" to cosmic proportions, celebrating the femininity of the *Erdgeist*, "the breasts of the world and the mystery of its belly." He imagined himself a fondled child, "the baby Rozanov lost somewhere on earth's breasts."[114] "I am like a child in his mother's womb, but one who doesn't wish to be born. 'I am warm enough here!' "[115]

This metaphor of maternal warmth is pervasive. "To lie in the warm sand after swimming is in its way worth any philosophy. And the *lazzaroni*, always lying in the sand, are a splendid school of philosophy."[116] It is clear that Rozanov associated warmth with life, family, God; and cold with godlessness, sexlessness, and death.

Religion," Rozanov insists, "should embrace everything . . . , what does not embrace everything is not religion. . . ."[117] Only in the churches, he adds, is it warm: "People have breathed in their warmth here."[118] Without the church the earth would "lose its meaning and grow cold."[119] "To me God is 'that which is warmest.' With God I am most warm. With God I am never bored or cold. . . ."[120]

[113] "Khristos i mir," in *Dukhovny krizis intelligentsii*, p. 236.
[114] *Opavshiye listya*, 2:439, *Izbrannoye*, pp. 377 f.
[115] *Uyedinyonnoye*, p. 128; *Solitaria*, p. 90.
[116] *Ibid.*, p. 207; *Solitaria*, p. 115.
[117] *Sredi khudozhnikov* [Among the Artists] (1914), pp. 168 f.
[118] *Uyedinyonnoye*, p. 248; *Solitaria*, p. 127.
[119] *Uyedinyonnoye*, p. 285; *Solitaria*, p. 139.
[120] *Uyedinyonnoye*, pp. 116 f.; *Solitaria*, p. 86.

Although he developed no theology, Rozanov, who sometimes suggested that he was a "God-seeker," had definite views about the nature of God. He insisted that God must be "a person, living, free."[121] He described his relationship to God as "I–thou." God, he declared, is "always close to me. My God is my peculiar one. He is only my God, and nobody else's yet. . . . 'My God' is boundless intimacy. . . ."[122]

Rozanov's religious mood, however, was not always so assured: "He who does not know sorrow," he once wrote, "does not know religion."[123] In the preface to the second volume of *By the Walls of the Church* he confessed that

I too love the sun, dry weather, and tranquility. But "since the Fall," it seems that we are condemned to wander and wander, in bad weather, in the rain—tired out, and walking toward a goal which we cannot see.[124]

Like Leontyev, Rozanov was a lonely and misunderstood but highly original religious thinker. He was also a supremely gifted writer, one of the most brilliant essayists and aphorists of the early twentieth century. Like Leontyev, he has long been virtually ignored, both as writer and thinker. Shestov and Berdyaev, to whom we turn in chapter 3, are much better known, Berdyaev especially. But, in my judgment Rozanov and Leontyev were Shestov's equals as writers and thinkers, and rather more than the equal of Berdyaev.

[121] *Okolo tserkovnykh sten*, 2:x, 452.
[122] *Uyedinyonnoye*, p. 118, and *Solitaria*, p. 87.
[123] *Opavshiye listya*, 2:48, and *Izbrannoye*, p. 321.
[124] *Okolo tserkovnykh sten*, 2:x.

3

RELIGIOUS EXISTENTIALISTS:
SHESTOV AND BERDYAEV

Shestov, ten years younger than Rozanov, published his first book in 1898, a dozen years after Rozanov's first book. Their periods of intellectual maturity and recognition as writers and thinkers overlapped by more than a decade (ca. 1905–19) but they were not personally acquainted, did not correspond with each other, and apparently did not even react to each other's work—except for two brief comments Shestov wrote long after Rozanov's death, in 1927 and 1930 (see note 1 below).

In contrast, Shestov's relations with his younger contemporary, Berdyaev (eight years his junior), were close and, on the whole, cordial. The two men knew each other over a period of at least thirty years, corresponded with some regularity, and often saw each other during the years they lived in the suburbs of Paris (1930–38). In 1938 each wrote a perceptive and appreciative, though not uncritical, essay on the thought of the other.

Both thinkers were "religious existentialists," centrally concerned with personal freedom, although Shestov was a more uncompromising and paradoxical "irrationalist" than Berdyaev. Both were heavily influenced by Dostoyevski, as well as by Nietzsche. Beyond that the influences diverged: Shestov was closest to Pascal, and in his last years to Kierkegaard. Berdyaev was closest to Böhme, and in some respects to Kant.

I

Shestov, born Lev Isaakovich Schwarzmann (Shvartsman) in 1866, was the son of a prosperous textile merchant and manufacturer of Kiev. He studied at *gymnasia* in Kiev and Moscow, and then at Moscow University, first in the Faculty of Mathematics and later in the Faculty of Law. Because of difficulties with the university authorities Shestov returned to Kiev and completed his education in law with the Candidate of Laws degree, roughly equivalent to the LL.M., in 1889. Shestov, however, never practiced law; he lived abroad, in Italy and Switzerland, from 1895 to 1898, and then returned briefly to St. Petersburg. He was abroad again, in Germany and Switzerland, from 1908 until 1914, when he returned to Moscow.

After the Bolshevik revolution Shestov moved to Kiev, and from there to Paris, arriving early in 1920. Except for the short periods he spent in Germany, he lived in or near Paris until his death, in November, 1938. Like Berdyaev, Shestov in his later years traveled relatively little. He gave occasional papers before philosophical associations or congresses in Berlin, Freiburg, Amsterdam, Prague, and Krakow. He made a lecture tour, in his seventieth year, to Palestine, and audiences in Jerusalem, Tel Aviv, and Haifa received him enthusiastically.[1]

Again like Berdyaev, Shestov was involved in editing a Russian émigré periodical. But Shestov's journal, Vyorsty [Mileposts], which he co-edited with the poetess Marina Tsvetayeva and the literary critic Prince Dimitri Sviatopolk-Mirsky, was

[1] The fullest biography of Shestov in English is to be found in Rabbi Bernard Martin's introduction to his translation of Shestov's *Athens and Jerusalem* (Athens, O.: Ohio University Press, 1966), pp. 15–27.

74

much shorter-lived than Berdyaev's journal *Put* [The Way].[2]

Shestov's first book was on Shakespeare, and in later writings he often referred to Shakespeare as his "first teacher of philosophy." (He interpreted Hamlet's enigmatic "The time is out of joint" as expressing a profound existential truth.) Shestov turned to philosophy relatively late, apparently around 1895, when he experienced a moral or spiritual crisis, although he himself never referred to such a crisis.[3] His works are far from being what Goethe had called his own writings, "fragments of a great confession"; in fact, they are less confessional and autobiographical than those of most existential thinkers. This does not mean, however, that they are impersonal or unimpassioned; intensity, passion, *engagement*—moral and religious rather than political—are hallmarks of Shestov's thought. Berdyaev expressed this aptly when he called Shestov a thinker who "philosophized with his whole being, for whom philosophy was not an academic specialty but a matter of life and death."[4]

Like Leontyev and Rozanov, Shestov was more directly involved with literary criticism than was Berdyaev. In addition to his book on Shakespeare he wrote penetrating critical essays on Tolstoy, Dostoyevski, and Chekhov.

All of Shestov's major works—those published between 1905

[2] In 1927 Shestov wrote an introductory note to a new edition of Rozanov's *Apocalypse of Our Time* (1918–19) that appeared in *Vyorsty*. Three years later he published a short article on Rozanov in Berdyaev's journal, *Put* (no. 22 [June, 1930], pp. 97–103).

[3] See Boris de Schloezer's "Un penseur russe: Léon Chestov," *Mercure de France*, 159 (1922):86. De Schloezer knew Shestov intimately for many years and translated most of his works from Russian into French.

[4] N. A. Berdyaev, "Osnovnaya ideya filosofii Lva Shestova" [The Fundamental Idea of Leon Shestov's Philosophy], *Put*, no. 58 (1938–39), p. 44. This article has been reprinted as an introduction to a posthumous collection of Shestov's essays, *Umozreniye i otkroveniye* [Speculation and Revelation] (Paris, 1964).

and 1938—are mosaics of brief, almost aphoristic essays, reminiscent of Pascal's *Pensées*, Nietzsche's *Beyond Good and Evil*, and Rozanov's *Solitaria* and *Fallen Leaves*. His style, often ironic and questioning, makes abundant use of paradoxical statement.

> People are offended [Shestov wrote] when I enunciate two contradictory propositions simultaneously. . . . But the difference between them and me is that I speak frankly of my contradictions while they prefer to conceal theirs, even to themselves. . . . They seem to think of contradictions as *pudenda* of the human spirit.[5]

In another place Shestov complained that Berdyaev had been unkind in exposing a contradiction in one of his early books.

> I must admit that Berdyaev has caught me. But why should he want to catch me? . . . Words and thoughts are only imperfect means of communication. It is impossible to photograph the soul . . . so we are obliged to use words. . . . But now Berdyaev tries to catch me. Instead of . . . realizing how impossible it is to find adequate expressions, coming to my aid, and guessing [my meaning], he thrusts a stick between the spokes of my wheels.[6]

Unlike Berdyaev, who wrote on a wide variety of topics (historical and political studies, intellectual biographies, a critique of Soviet philosophy, an essay on anti-Semitism), Shestov—at least after 1905—wrote essentially on only one theme: religion and ethics, or the religious basis of human values. He attacked one target—the idea of rational necessity—in metaphysics, ethics, and philosophical theology.

[5] *Vlast klyuchei* [The Power of the Keys] (Berlin, 1923), p. 114.

[6] "Pokhvala gluposti" [The Praise of Folly], in *Nachala i kontsy* [Beginnings and Endings] (St. Petersburg, 1908), p. 121. Earlier, Shestov had written that "there are things about which one can think but about which it is impossible to speak except in symbols and hints" (*Dostoyevski i Nitshe: Filosofiya tragedii* [Dostoyevski and Nietzsche: The Philosophy of Tragedy] (St. Petersburg, 1903), p. 133).

Shestov, a rather more polemical thinker than Berdyaev, offers explicit and devastating criticisms of rival positions, particularly of the various species of "rationalism" in philosophy and religion. He tends, however, to suggest rather than assert or argue his own position. Berdyaev once declared that Shestov's strength was "in his negation, not in his affirmation, in his yearning for faith, and not in his faith."[7] Shestov, in the words of another critic, cultivated a "respect for mystery" and put emphasis on "unique and mystical experience," on the personal and even "ecstatic," which is reminiscent of Hassidic Judaism.[8]

Shestov's fundamental "either/or" is formulated in the title of his major work on the philosophy of religion, *Athens and Jerusalem*. Athens stands for reason, rationality, and the insistence on an orderly, fully knowable cosmos, ruled by necessary and eternal laws that even God could not modify. Jerusalem is the city of biblical faith, of an existential irrationalism that stresses contingency, arbitrariness, mystery, "pure possibility."

Shestov was, in a sense, a "biblical thinker"; but, as Berdyaev pointed out in 1936, he was highly selective in his reading of scripture: he stressed the story of the Fall, Abraham and Isaac, and the Book of Job—neglecting Moses and "the law."[9] In 1939 Father Bulgakov said that, although Shestov failed to recognize it, "Athens" was in fact a school of *Christian* theology and "Jerusalem" was not entirely a stranger to *thought*. Thus

[7] Berdyaev, "Lev Shestov i Kirkegaard" [Leon Shestov and Kierkegaard], *Russkiye Zapiski*, 62 (1936):378.

[8] See Sidney Monas, introduction to a new edition of Shestov's *Chekhov and Other Essays* (Ann Arbor, Mich.: University of Michigan Press, 1966), pp. viii–ix.

[9] "Lev Shestov i Kirkegaard," p. 377.

Shestov's "either/or," Bulgakov suggests, should have been a "both/and."[10]

For God, as Shestov never tires of repeating, "all things are possible," even things the rationalist Descartes had called logically contradictory; namely, making what had in fact happened not to have happened.[11] Shestov notes that in the Middle Ages, when Peter Damian asserted that God could make what had been not to have been, his was "the voice of one crying in the wilderness."[12]

Berdyaev perceptively remarks that Shestov "was tormented by the inevitability [neotvratimost; Berdyaev should have said nevozvratimost, 'irrevocability'] of the past, the horror of that which has once happened (odnazhdy byvshevo)."[13] There are four fateful and irrevocable events to which Shestov constantly recurs (although the fourth event appears only in the writings of his last decade): Job's loss of his children, the poisoning of Socrates, Nietzsche's mental illness, and Kierkegaard's giving up Regina Olsen. It is in God's power, Shestov insists, to make those who have died not to have died, as when Job's children—the same children, not a new generation—were restored to him at the end of the biblical story. It is within God's power to undo the "eternal truth" that Socrates was poisoned; that is, Socrates could retroactively, so to speak, not have been poisoned after all.

[10] S. N. Bulgakov, "Nekotoryie cherty religioznovo mirovozzreniya L. I. Shestova" [Some Features of the Religious World View of L. I. Shestov], Sovremennyie Zapiski, 68 (1939):312.

[11] This phrase, which Shestov quoted long before he had read Kierkegaard, who also liked to quote it, is from Mark 10:27: "With men it is impossible, but not with God: for with God all things are possible" (Para anthrōpois adynaton, all'ou para tō Theō: panta gar dynata esti para tō Theō).

[12] Afiny i Ierusalim (Paris, 1951), p. 17, and Athens and Jerusalem, p. 63.

[13] "Osnovnaya ideya," p. 46.

Berdyaev protested that, in the case of Kierkegaard, it may have been God Himself and not a heartless "rational necessity" that took Regina away, and that this may have been "for the best" because otherwise Kierkegaard might not have written his brilliant works. Shestov could have replied that this loss, even if it was "for the best" for Kierkegaard's readers, was a doubtful blessing for Kierkegaard himself.

In any case it is clear that, for rationalists, all such Damian-like claims are simply incoherent; what has happened cannot be made—even by God—not to have happened. As Aristotle liked to say, we are "forced by the truth itself" to admit that, once Socrates has taken the hemlock, it will always and necessarily be the case that he did so.

Shestov's "revolt against reason," as it has been called, reached its extreme in the assertion that God can revoke the past, but he repudiated "rational necessities" of other kinds as well. For both philosophical and theological rationalists, he noted, there is an eternal structure of being, a system of eternal laws—as Spinoza and Kant had insisted—prior to all lawgivers and to all acts of cosmic legislation. "Both before and after Kant," Shestov declared, "the eternal truths have continued to blaze above us like fixed stars, and we frail mortals, thrown down into infinite time and space, have oriented ourselves by them."[14]

Shestov frequently quoted Seneca's saying: "*Ipse creator et conditor mundi semel jussit; semper paret*" ("The creator and founder of the world decreed but once; he obeys forever").[15] In Shestov's interpretation, in fact, rationalists admit not even the one-time decree of Seneca's *semel jussit*; the "decree" is timeless or eternal. The decree has always been in effect, which is to say that there never was an act of decreeing. "The creator,"

[14] *Afiny*, p. 12, and *Athens*, p. 55.
[15] Seneca *De Providentia* 5. 8 (italics added in the English translation).

Shestov wrote, "as well as all rational and non-rational creatures, have always *obeyed*."[16] Unquestioning acceptance of objective laws, as formulated in the truths of pure reason, this —for Shestov—is the heart of philosophical rationalism.

Necessary objective *laws* say, in effect, "Thou shalt" and "Thou shalt not"; they demand obedience. Non-necessary, arbitrary, subjective *decrees* say, in effect, "Let it be so" or "It need not be so." For Shestov, both species of non-necessity—namely, natural contingency and human or divine arbitrariness—make possible free choice, decision, and creativity.

Universal and necessary norms, norms that are what Kant called *allgemeingültig* ("universally valid"), limit and repress free creativity. For Shestov as for Nietzsche, "all life is creative *tolma* ["daring" or "audacity"] and therefore an eternal mystery, irreducible to anything finished or intelligible." We naturally (i.e., "rationally") fear chaos as a loss or deficiency of order. In fact, Shestov insists, "chaos is not a limited possibility, but the direct opposite, an unlimited opportunity."[17] Earlier he had written—very much in the spirit of Berdyaev—that "the first and essential condition of life is lawlessness. Laws are a refreshing sleep—lawlessness is creative activity."[18]

In Dostoyevski's *Notes from the Underground*, the first part of which Shestov found both congenial and profound, "necessity" is symbolized by the "stone wall" and "twice two is four." Against both of these "truths of reason" the man from the

[16] "In Memory of a Great Philosopher: Edmund Husserl," trans. George L. Kline, in *Russian Philosophy*, ed. James M. Edie, James P. Scanlan, Mary-Barbara Zeldin, and George L. Kline (Chicago: Quadrangle Books, 1965), 3:261.

[17] L. I. Shestov, *In Job's Balances* (New York, 1932), pp. 158, 226.

[18] *All Things Are Possible*, trans. S. S. Koteliansky (London and New York, 1920), p. 127; the original work is *Apofeoz bespochvennosti* [The Apotheosis of Groundlessness] (St. Petersburg, 1905).

underground "absurdly" rebels. Shestov credits Dostoyevski with having intuitively recognized that "things do not exist 'necessarily' but 'freely.' "[19]

It might be objected that Shestov confused two distinct senses of law: descriptive law (law of nature) and prescriptive law (norm or edict). There is some validity in such an objection, but I think that Shestov's point could be reformulated, in light of this distinction, without being seriously weakened. Shestov could say, with Kant, that descriptive laws, insofar as the regularities they describe are universal and necessary, not merely local or statistical, state not only what *is* but also what *must be* the case. Thus they function as "prescriptions" in the sense that they make unrefusable demands. Ordinary prescriptive laws, whether moral or legal, are neither universal nor necessary in this sense, although Kant, for one, held them to be. The demands they make, as even Kant admitted, are not unrefusable.

For Kant, of course, descriptive laws "coerce" and moral laws "persuade," but both are *allgemeingültig*. The "natural necessity" of the one kind of law is matched by the "moral necessity" of the other kind. It is precisely this character of *Allgemeingültigkeit*, of universal validity or bindingness, that Shestov was concerned to repudiate. He would say, I think, that the "free decree" of the Senecan *jubere* does not lay claim to universal validity, does not make (either refusable or unrefusable) demands.

Shestov, in his late discussion of Husserl, speaks not only of universal and necessary truths but also of "self-evidence" or "self-evident truth" (*ochevidnost*, in translation of Husserl's

[19] Quoted in Monas, introduction to Shestov's *Chekhov and Other Essays*, p. vii.

term *Evidenz*). Self-evident truth, he declares, "is like a Medusa's head: everyone who looks at it is rendered spiritually impotent, turned to stone, paralyzed in will so as to submit to every influence from without."[20] In other words it makes demands that are unrefusable, and intolerable.

Obedience to objective necessity means acquiescence in the "horrors of existence," horrors expressed by "the cries of Job, the lamentations of Jeremiah, the thundering of the Apocalypse." Men accept theoretical truth even when it encroaches upon "what is most precious to them, upon what they consider sacred." Truths are truths, Shestov complains, "whether or not men need them, whether men (and even gods) are gladdened or saddened by them, filled with hope or with despair."[21]

In terms of the story of the Fall, which Shestov liked to repeat, the Serpent lied when he promised Adam and Eve that if they ate of the fruit of the tree of knowledge they would be like God. Theoretical truth does not make men like God or the gods; rather, it makes God or the gods like men, equally subject to necessary and universal truth.

The rationalist position is stated with radical clarity by Husserl, who declared: "What is true is absolutely true, is true 'in itself.' Truth is identically one, whether it be apprehended in the judgments of men or monsters (*Menschen oder Unmenschen*), of angels or of gods."[22] Reason commands; man must obey. *Roma locuta, causa finita* (Rome has spoken, the case is closed); but for Shestov, when reason speaks the case is far from closed. Theoretical reason is destructive of human values and hence must be resolutely opposed.

[20] "In Memory of a Great Philosopher," in *Russian Philosophy*, 3:263.
[21] *Ibid.*, pp. 264, 276.
[22] Edmund Husserl, *Logische Untersuchungen* (1900), 1:117; quoted by Shestov in "In Memory of a Great Philosopher," in *Russian Philosophy*, 3:256.

Man wants to think in the categories in which he lives, and not to live in the categories in which he has been taught to think: the tree of knowledge shall no longer deaden the tree of life.

In Shestov's view, knowledge is "subjugation, deprivation," which in the last analysis threatens to turn man into a "thinking stone." Shestov here refers to Spinoza's falling stone that would, if it were able to think, assume that it was falling freely, of its own "free will," and would of course be mistaken because, like everything else, it would be acting from eternal and unalterable necessity. At just this point, however, where according to reason "all possibilities have already been exhausted, everything is finished, [and] nothing remains for man but to look and grow cold," Shestov is ready (with Kierkegaard) to begin the "mad struggle for the possible"; that is, the struggle to make the impossible possible.[23] This is the central task of existential philosophy and the central reality of religious faith.

This desperate struggle is marked by "madness" or "folly" only in the sense that "man's wisdom is folly in the sight of the Lord," in the words of scripture that both Kierkegaard and Shestov frequently cited. The task of existential philosophy is to "teach men to live in ignorance or uncertainty (neizvestnost)," to swim, as Kierkegaard had put it, "above the seventy thousand fathoms." As Shestov wrote in another place, "It is when a man comes to feel the utter impossibility of living with reason that faith first arises in him."[24] It is reason, not faith, that demands obedience and submission. Faith, as we have seen, permits and nourishes freedom; faith is itself an "unfathomable creative force."

[23] "In Memory of a Great Philosopher," in Russian Philosophy, 3:265.
[24] Quoted in B. Griftsov, Tri myslitelya: V. Rozanov, D. Merezhkovski, L. Shestov [Three Thinkers: V. Rozanov, D. Merezhkovski, L. Shestov] (Moscow, 1911), p. 187.

According to Shestov, men can live with and by faith, but they cannot live with or by reason because the absolutization of theoretical truth is inevitably a relativization, and degradation, of life—of human existence. Shestov was quite prepared to move in the opposite direction—to relativize, and even degrade, theoretical truth in order to absolutize moral and religious values, and thus "save" or "redeem" the existing individual.

The point may be expressed in terms of the rich and ambiguous Russian word *pravda*, which means both theoretical truth (*istina*) and practical justice (*spravedlivost*), or "truth-justice." Rationalists such as Tolstoy assume that theoretical truth (*pravda-istina*) can and should serve as a support for practical justice (*pravda-spravedlivost*) in individual and social life. In 1908 Shestov had quoted Mikhailovski's hymn to the harmonious combination of these two aspects of *pravda*, commenting that for the early Berdyaev no less than for Mikhailovski there is a "moral order of the world which fully corresponds to man's conceptions of what should and should not be, of what is desirable and what is undesirable."[25]

In contrast, Shestov insists that moral values, or the humanly valued (here symbolized by *pravda-spravedlivost*), must take—or rather retake—priority, displacing or denying the claims of theoretical truth (*pravda-istina*) in all cases of conflict. And it was Shestov's special insight—or obsession—that the cases of conflict are frequent and total, inasmuch as there is no such thing as the "moral order of the world"—or coincidence of *pravda-istina* and *pravda-spravedlivost*—that rationalists assume.

One of the "eternal and self-evident truths" against which Shestov rebelled is the assumption, which he traced back to Anaximander, that whatever is born must die, that coming-

[25] "Pokhvala gluposti," in *Nachala i kontsy*, pp. 115 f.

to-be (in Greek, *genesis*) is a kind of affront to the gods, an act of cosmic *hubris*, which must be punished by ceasing-to-be or perishing (*phthora*). According to Shestov, rationalists find in the very notion of existence "something improper, a defect, sickness, or sin."[26] Even Nietzsche ended with a preaching of *amor fati*, a submissive love of fateful necessity, including the necessity of perishing.[27] Nietzsche too accepted Anaximander's dictum, although (we may add) he awkwardly attempted to "overcome" or transcend man's necessary finitude through the incoherent hypothesis of a cosmic "eternal recurrence."

Shestov liked to quote Pascal's question "Who will make the sorrows of Job weigh more heavily than the sands of the sea?" With Kierkegaard, he insisted that there are scales—"Job's balances"—upon which human suffering and death do outweigh the "stone-like, fateful" necessities of nature. And it is on Job's balances, not on the balances of speculative philosophy, that man's fate must be weighed.

What are the "unendurable horrors of existence" to which Shestov so often refers? The expression first occurs explicitly in his two early books on Nietzsche (1900 and 1903); he was obviously impressed by what Nietzsche had said in *The Birth of Tragedy* (1872) about the "horrors and atrocities of existence" (*Schrecken und Entsetzlichkeiten des Daseins*). He had, however, given vivid examples of all this in his own first book,

---

[26] *Kirgegard i ekzistentsialnaya filosofiya* [Kierkegaard and Existential Philosophy] (Paris, 1939), p. 8. (An English translation, by Mrs. Elinor Hewitt, is in the press.)

[27] Shestov's appropriation of Nietzsche's thought—like his appropriation of the thought of his other intellectual heroes: Tertullian, Luther, Pascal, Kierkegaard, even Dostoyevski—was highly selective. One of Shestov's earliest critics, reviewing his 1900 book on Tolstoy and Nietzsche, pointed out that Shestov ignored such characteristic Nietzschean themes as the will to power, the "pathos of distance," and the *Übermensch* (N. K. Mikhailovski, *Russkoye Bogatstvo*, no. I [1900], pp. 156 f).

on Shakespeare (1898), in discussing the sufferings of Lear, Gloucester, and Cordelia, and especially in attacking the uninvolved "objectivism" of the critic Taine.

Not long ago a cemetery guard was caught in the act of desecrating corpses. But don't be horrified: the sum of the angles of a triangle is equal to two right angles. Not long ago a certain man's only son was killed in battle. But never mind: the diagonal is greater than the perpendicular.[28]

In 1905 Shestov added: "We pause in panic and perplexity at the sight of deformity, disease, insanity, poverty, old age, death."[29]

In his later writings Shestov tended to be less specific and more allusive. He referred to the horrors described by Ivan in Dostoyevski's *Brothers Karamazov*, the unbearable suffering of innocent children. In his last works Shestov evoked biblical archetypes: "the horrors which Job suffered, the horrors which Jeremiah lamented, the horrors of which John thundered in his revelation."[30] *Either* the "eternal truths" of reason are only temporary and transitory, Shestov declares, in which case all such horrors will be

turned into nothing, into an illusion, by the will of Him who created the universe and "all that dwell therein," just as the horrors of a nightmare which absolutely dominates the consciousness of the sleeping man turn into nothing when he awakens—or we live in a world of madness.[31]

Shestov had used a similar metaphor earlier, when he declared that "only death and the madness of death are able to awaken

[28] *Shekspir i yevo kritik Brandes* [Shakespeare and His Critic Brandes] (St. Petersburg, 1898), p. 14.
[29] *Apoteoz bespochvennosti*, p. 66, and *All Things are Possible*, p. 69.
[30] In Memory of a Great Philosopher," in *Russian Philosophy*, 3:273.
[31] *Loc. cit.*

man from the nightmare of existence."[32] In a letter to Berdyaev
he added: "Only the experience of death or an equivalent experience of tragedy . . . opens man's eyes to the vanity of all earthly
privileges (*privilegii*), including those of morality."[33] By 'privileges' Shestov appears to mean "general principles having a
privileged status"; for example, Kant's categorical imperative,
which he elsewhere forcefully attacks.

He reminds us that Kierkegaard had faced a "shattering
dilemma: in order to find God he had to overcome reason and
suspend the ethical."[34] It seems clear that Shestov was describ-
ing not only Kierkegaard's dilemma but his own as well. And
Shestov, no less than Kierkegaard, used the tools of reason to
combat reason. As Berdyaev put it, "He struggled against the
tyranny of reason, against the power of knowledge . . . on the
territory of knowledge itself, resorting to the weapons of reason
itself."[35]

Shestov's "either/or"—*either* "rational necessity" and the horrors of existence which it certifies and legitimizes or a faith
that promises salvation from those horrors—is not a choice, as
rationalists would say, between reason and unreason, between
sanity and insanity. It is an "absurd," existential choice between
two kinds of insanity. Shestov's distinction is to a degree reminiscent of the distinction Kierkegaard had drawn between
"objective" and "subjective" madness. There is, on the one
hand, the insanity of theoretical reason, which accepts as ultimate, eternal, and inevitable the objective truths that "rational-
ize" and legitimize man's finitude, suffering, and mortality. On

[32] *In Job's Balances*, p. 93.

[33] Paris, 1924, in *Mosty* (New York), 8 (1961):257.

[34] "N. Berdyaev: Gnozis i ekzistentsialnaya filosofiya," *Sovremennyie
Zapiski*, 67 (1938):227.

[35] "Osnovnaya ideya," pp. 47 f.

the other hand is the insanity of the "leap of faith," the desperate struggle against these self-evident and necessary truths.

Shestov is close to the Lutheran conception of "salvation by faith alone" (*sola fide*); in fact, the Latin phrase appears as the title of his posthumously published study (French edition 1956, Russian edition 1966) of Luther and medieval philosophy. However, as Berdyaev remarked, Shestov sometimes gives the impression that only Abraham had faith in this "maximalist" sense.[36] "Freedom," Shestov wrote, "comes to man not from knowledge, but from faith, which puts an end to all our fears."[37]

Shestov's many references to Job and Abraham (and also to Isaiah, although, interestingly enough, he makes few references to Ecclesiastes) have given rise to the assumption that his is exclusively an "Old Testament faith." Berdyaev, for example, accused him of not appreciating the New Testament, of not grasping the significance of the Incarnation, and of rejecting the Passion as a limitation upon God's omnipotence.

Shestov rejected the alternative. In one of his last letters, to Father Serge Bulgakov, he declared that the opposition between the Old and the New Testament had always struck him as "illusory." He referred to Mark 12:29: "And Jesus answered him, The first of all the commandments is, Hear, O Israel, The Lord our God is one Lord." This "one Lord," Shestov insists, is proclaimed by both the Old and the New Testament, and it is these "good tidings" alone that give us the strength to face the "horrors of life."[38] As for Berdyaev's charge that he had neglected the doctrine of the Incarnation, Shestov responded: "In our veil of tears, the consciousness that God has shared our sorrows and sufferings brings us great relief and consolation. . . ."[39]

---

[36] "Lev Shestov i Kirkegaard," p. 378.

[37] "N. Berdyayev," p. 229.

[38] Boulon sur Seine, October 26, 1938, in *Mosty*, 8 (1961):260.

[39] "N. Berdyayev," p. 219.

"To deliver oneself into the hands of the living God," Shestov exclaimed with irony, "is dreadful, but to submit to an impersonal necessity, which has laid its grip on existence, no one knows how, is not dreadful but joyful and reassuring!"[40] At the same time Shestov emphasized that, because for God there is no boundary between what to human reason is possible and what is impossible, God does not "take into account" either human rationality or human morality. "Can one entrust his fate to God without having first been convinced that God is a rational and moral being?"[41] Shestov's answer, of course, is a ringing affirmative, and at the same time a clear denial of Plato's claim (in the Euthyphro) that a thing is loved by the gods because it is holy rather than that it is holy because it is loved by the gods. The criterion of holiness, and more generally of value, is not—as Plato had held—objective; it is subjective and "existential."

Shestov's final profession of Kierkegaardian faith involves the claim that, because "for God all things are possible" and because "God cares for each living human being," the "ultimate victory lies not with the iniquities and inexorabilities of reality, but with a God Who 'numbers the hairs upon a man's head,' a loving God, Who promises that every tear shall be wiped away."[42]

The above words were among the last that Shestov wrote. They were published posthumously, in his long article "In Memory of a Great Philosopher," devoted to Edmund Husserl, who had died only a few months earlier. The very title, and Shestov's generous praise of his chief intellectual opponent

---

[40] Afiny, p. 12, and Athens, p. 55.

[41] Kirgegard i ekzistentsialnaya filosofiya, p. 68.

[42] "In Memory of a Great Philosopher," in Russian Philosophy, 3:271.

among twentieth-century thinkers, is characteristic of Shestov —but hard to imagine in Tolstoy and, I think, even in Berdyaev.

Shestov's generosity and largeness of spirit seem to me unique among existential thinkers, most of whom—including the brilliant, often perverse, and sometimes profound Kierkegaard— have been jealous of their subjectivity, proud of their suffering, and ungenerous toward the thinkers from whom they have learned most.

II

Berdyaev once called himself, using a term originally applied to Nietzsche, an "aristocratic radical," and it seems clear that there was something aristocratic about his religious and philosophic attitude. Like Herzen and Leontyev, he found middle-class "Philistine" existence aesthetically and morally repulsive. As he himself revealingly expressed it, he went through life "holding his nose."[43] Combined with a romantic exaltation of creative genius, this aristocratic *hauteur* found philosophical expression in Berdyaev's central categories of person, spirit, freedom, and creativity, and (negatively) in his *bête noire*, "objectification" (*obyektivizatsiya*).

Nikolai Aleksandrovich Berdyaev, born in the Ukraine in 1874 into a family of the landed gentry, attended a military school and studied law at Kiev University. Still a student, he was arrested for radical activities and exiled to Vologda (1900–3), where his exile was shared by Lunacharski. Berdyaev never completed his formal education, although in later years he read widely and deeply in philosophical and theological literature, both Russian and Western.

[43] N. A. Berdyaev, *Dream and Reality*, trans. K. Lampert (London, 1950; New York, 1951), p. 21.

Intellectually, Berdyaev moved from the "Populist" (*Narodnik*) social philosophy of Lavrov and Mikhailovski to Marxism, which in the mid-1890's attracted many of the most sensitive and intelligent young Russians. By 1902, however, he had abandoned Marxism, which he had never taken straight but always with a strong admixture of Kantian ethics and theory of knowledge, in favor of a pure Kantianism.[44] As Shestov noted in 1908, Berdyaev's theoretical doubts did not touch the "granite of faith" in the depth of his soul. He raised doubts whether Marx or Kant or Merezhkovski was right, "but he was always convinced that, whichever side the truth turned out to be on, it would have a consoling . . . character."[45] Within a decade Berdyaev largely abandoned Kant in favor of Dostoyevski, Nietzsche, and his own form of religious existentialism.

In 1922 Berdyaev was expelled from the Soviet Union, along with a number of other non- and anti-Marxist intellectuals, and forbidden to return on pain of death. He lived first in Berlin, and then, from the end of 1923, in France, where he settled in the Paris suburb of Clamart, remaining there until his death in 1948.

In Paris Berdyaev edited *Put* (*The Path* or *The Way*), a journal of religious and philosophical thought, from 1925 to 1940, and he collaborated closely with the Russian-language YMCA Press, which published works by such exiled thinkers as Shestov, S. L. Frank, V. V. Zenkovsky, K. V. Mochulski, and Berdyaev himself. Berdyaev produced a torrent of books and articles, most of which were quickly translated from Rus-

---

[44] I have discussed Berdyaev's "Kantian-Marxist" ethical theory of 1901 in "Theoretische Ethik im russischen Frühmarxismus," *Forschungen zur osteuropäischen Geschichte*, 9 (1963):270–74. See also my chapter, "Leszek Kołakowski and the Revision of Marxism," in *European Philosophy Today*, ed. George L. Kline (Chicago: Quadrangle Books, 1965), esp. pp. 132–34.

[45] "Pokhvala gluposti," p. 112.

sian into the major West European languages. His intellectual autobiography, published posthumously in 1949, was titled: *Samopoznaniye: opyt filosofskoi avtobiografii* [Self-Knowledge: An Essay in Philosophical Autobiography] and, in the abridged and heavily edited English translation, *Dream and Reality*.

Berdyaev, like Shestov in his last works, was quite willing to call himself an "existentialist" thinker. He insisted, however, that he stood in the "true" existentialist tradition of St. Augustine, Pascal, Kierkegaard (with some reservations), and Nietzsche (with further reservations), rather than in the (presumably "pseudo-existentialist") tradition of Heidegger, Jaspers, and Sartre.

In his critique of "bourgeois Philistinism" (*meshchanstvo*) Berdyaev drew heavily upon both Herzen and Leontyev. His doctrine of freedom was most strongly influenced by Dostoyevski, Kant, and Schelling. His mystical doctrine of the *Ungrund*, "the abyss of non-being," comes from Jakob Böhme.

As the above names suggest, Berdyaev was a somewhat eclectic thinker, at least when compared to the single-minded Shestov or, for that matter, the single-minded Leontyev or Rozanov. But this does not mean that his thought was unoriginal. Some of his themes in philosophy of religion and philosophical theology are so "original" as to have brought charges of heresy from his Russian Orthodox colleagues.

Berdyaev, in a letter to Shestov, lamented his "strange lot": "Left-wingers consider me right-wing, right-wingers consider me left-wing; the orthodox consider me a heretic, the heretics consider me orthodox." He added that he found "Bolshevik obscurantism" and "right-wing obscurantism" equally repugnant.[46]

[46] Berlin, 1924, in *Mosty*, 8 (1961):258.

Unlike Shestov, Berdyaev had a penchant for Hegelian, or quasi-Hegelian, generalizations formulated in terms of large historical triads. Thus in the realm of ethics and social philosophy he saw a dialectic that begins with a Renaissance individualism and leads to its own negation by socialist collectivism. The negation of that negation, according to Berdyaev, will be a Christian or "personalistic" socialism, which will preserve whatever is of value in each of the preceding stages—or, in Hegelian language, the earlier and now *aufgehobene Momente*. In such a socialism the "abstract individualism" of capitalism as well as the "abstract collectivism" of communism will be overcome and superseded in a concrete communalism or *sobornost*.[47]

A related Hegelian triad: the medieval period, Berdyaev says, was marked by belief in God without belief in man. Since the Renaissance there has been belief in man without belief in God. Now, in "Dostoyevskian Christianity," belief in man is harmoniously combined ("synthesized"?) with belief in God.

This seems much too neat to be true, and strongly reminiscent of Khomyakov's equally neat triadic *Aufhebung* of Catholicism and Protestantism in Russian Orthodoxy. The first, Khomyakov had said, represents unity without freedom, the second freedom without unity, and the third, of course, unity-in-freedom or freedom-in-unity.

Berdyaev sees a similarly triadic development in the realm of religious life and thought. Like Joachim of Flora in the high Middle Ages, he divided history into three stages, corresponding to the three persons of the Trinity. What Flora had called the age of the Father, Berdyaev calls the "epoch of law" (corresponding to the Old Testament). The age of the Son is, for

[47] Berdyaev, *The End of Our Time*, trans. Donald Attwater (London, 1933), pp. 196, 38.

93

Berdyaev, the "epoch of redemption" (the New Testament). The age of the Holy Spirit is the "epoch of creative spirit," presumably going beyond both the Old and the New Testament.

This triad is less obviously Hegelian than the others; the epoch of law is not *aufgehoben*, it is simply surpassed and left behind in the epoch of creative spirit. Even the epoch of redemption seems to have no clear place in the third epoch, as Berdyaev described it.

We should perhaps add that, like the age of "personalistic socialism," the "epoch of creative spirit"—according to Berdyaev—is just beginning. As it progresses, he asserts, it will be seen to involve not only God's self-revelation to man but also "man's self-revelation to God."

Shestov saw in this radical claim, and in Berdyaev's view of man as "co-creator" with God, a position that threatened to change from an initially theistic doctrine of God-manhood (*Bogochelovechestvo*) to a final "humanistic" and Promethean doctrine of Man-godhood (*chelovekobozhestvo*). Berdyaev's doctrine of God, Shestov claims, has become empty and thin, as his doctrine of man has become richer and fuller.[48] In other words, Shestov interprets Berdyaev as coming dangerously close to the secular Prometheanism of the Russian "God-builders" (see chapter 4 below).

According to Berdyaev, the end of the third epoch (of "creative spirit") will be the final *eschaton*, the "end of history" and the "end of time."

Berdyaev's broad distinction between the ethics and religion of law and the ethics and religion of love throws partial light on the differences between his stages. However, because both the second and the third epochs are marked by the ethics and

[48] "N. Berdyayev," p. 198.

94

religion of love, the difference between these epochs is not *prima facie* clear.

Berdyaev seems to want to distinguish between *redemptive* and *creative* love. (In an early work he had even spoken of Christian *eros*, rejecting Christian charity, *agapē*—although he does not use the Greek term—as "cold" and "dead.")[49] Redemptive love is "Christ's love for man"; creative love is the love with which each free spirit responds to the divine creative and redemptive love. Man is a co-creator with God. Berdyaev's theological doctrine of love here merges with his metaphysical doctrine of creativity.[50]

The figure of Christ in Dostoyevski's "Legend of the Grand Inquisitor," which Berdyaev called "one of the most revolutionary works in world literature," represents a synthesis, or fusion, of the two kinds of love. The figure is a suffering and compassionate Christ (an embodiment of redemptive love), but it is this Dostoyevskian Christ who insists, against the powerful rational arguments of the grand inquisitor, that men must never be deprived of their creative freedom.

We may note that Berdyaev used Dostoyevski's "Legend" rather than the New Testament as authority for most of his interpretations of the figure of Christ. Like Tolstoy, Berdyaev accepted only those New Testament doctrines that support his own view of God. In Berdyaev's case this means a being that is non-omnipotent, in process, suffering, and subject to tragic conflict.

We have seen (pp. 32–33) that Berdyaev rejected Tolstoy's

---

[49] *Novoye religioznoye soznaniye i obshchestvennost* [The New Religious Consciousness and Society] (St. Petersburg, 1907), pp. 169–71.

[50] A useful systematic compilation of Berdyaev's writings on philosophy of religion and philosophical theology is *Christian Existentialism: A Berdyaev Anthology*, selected and annotated by Donald A. Lowrie (London and New York, 1965).

"law of love" as a contradiction in terms. The kind of Christian love he accepts is not Tolstoyan but Dostoyevskian: the love of a Sonya Marmaladova, a Prince Myshkin, an Alyosha Karamazov, or, of course, the Christ of the "Legend." Such love is mysterious and "irrationally" sacrificial, sustained only by a powerful sense of the "living presence of God."

For Berdyaev, Christianity is the religion of love in this sense, and of creative freedom; but no power, human or divine, can force men to be either creative or free.[51] Berdyaev insists that the mode of divine influence is limited to love and persuasion. Force is ruled out, not because God refuses to use it but because He does not have it to use.

Berdyaev explicitly denies the applicability of the "categories of power and domination" either to "God or to God's relation to man and the world." Such categories, he says, are "sociomorphic," and not properly theological. "God has no power: he has less power than a policeman. . . . God can reconcile man to the suffering of creation because he himself suffers. . . ."[52] In some places Berdyaev goes so far as to imply that God is not only non-omnipotent but also non-active, as when he writes: "[God] determines nothing. . . . He is not the cause of anything."[53] To the more orthodox among the Orthodox this denial of God's omnipotence sounded dangerously like Manicheanism.

This contention also was a main point of difference between Berdyaev and Shestov. As we have seen, Shestov insisted that "all things are possible" for God. And he was quick to point

[51] There is an intriguing parallel between the Christ of Dostoyevski's "Legend" and Pasternak's Yuri Zhivago, the latter representing the fusion of what Pasternak called "sacrificial love" and "creative freedom."

[52] *Dream and Reality*, pp. 158, 179.

[53] *Slavery and Freedom*, trans. R. M. French (London, 1943; New York, 1944), p. 83.

out that, in Berdyaev's view, many things are impossible for God.[54]

One of the realities that God did not create, according to Berdyaev, is man's freedom. Man, of course, did not create it either. Freedom, as Böhme and Schelling had said, is "uncreated"; it is the Ungrund, the void or abyss of non-being. But this non-being is "meonic" (from the Greek me-on) rather than "oukonic" (from ouk-on, "absolute nothingness"). In Berdyaev's language, freedom is not "ontal" but "meonic."[55]

It seems to me that there is little in this formula—and in Sartre's related definition of freedom as the néantisation or "nihilation" of the en-soi by the pour-soi—beyond a confused and confusing restatement of the plain and ancient truth that the object of free choice is a possibility rather than an actuality, that decision and action involve the actualization of what is merely potential. Possibilities, of course, are non-actual, but— pace Sartre and Berdyaev—they are not nothing, not "non-being"—whether ouk or me!

Freedom, for Berdyaev, means "freedom from the world," the avoidance or overcoming of an "objectification" which involves some of the features Shestov had attacked: universality, necessity, coerciveness, and of course "objectivity." Berdyaev found the "objectified world" alien, hostile, and "intolerably banal," lacking in "spiritual freedom" and "spiritual mystery." And he sees it as totally transcended by the free creative activity of the human spirit.

The Kantian contrast between subjective (noumenal) freedom and objective (phenomenal) necessity is strikingly ex-

[54] "N. Berdyayev," p. 222.

[55] Schelling had formulated the distinction between me-on and ouk-on. In Russian philosophy both Chaadayev and Solovyov had used it before Berdyaev took it over.

pressed in the original Russian title of one of Berdyaev's major works (which in translation is called *Solitude and Society*): *Ya i mir obyektov*, literally "I and the World of Objects." The "I" is a person; the "objects" are non-persons; and the process of objectification is a depersonalizing process. The world of objects—not just sticks and stones but social institutions and human roles and relationships—appears to Berdyaev as a threat, an obstacle to "free spiritual creativity."

Following but, I think, somewhat vulgarizing Solovyov, Berdyaev sometimes asserted that the objectified and (spatio-temporally) externalized world is a cosmic product of man's fall. "The 'given world,' " he declared, "this phantom 'world' is born of our sin."[56]

Leaving aside this rather strange neo-Platonic or Schellingian doctrine, we must note that Berdyaev failed to face the theoretical difficulties involved in the notion of creativity as a purely spiritual activity whose products exist *only* in an objectified world that is nevertheless utterly alien to spirit. It would seem that Berdyaev's creativity is doomed not only to "partial and fragmentary embodiment" (to use his own words) but, because of its necessary involvement in the "objective world," to inescapable frustration. Berdyaev seems almost to admit as much when he refers, in another connection, to the "tragic failure of every outward action."[57]

God, according to Berdyaev, is unobjectified and unobjectifiable, and hence, strictly speaking, unconceptualizable and unknowable. (This is the "truth" which he finds in negative —"apophatic"—theology.) As the mystics saw, God stands "beyond being," beyond ontological categories. ". . . the limit-

[56] *The Meaning of the Creative Act*, trans. Donald A. Lowrie (London and New York, 1955), p. 11.

[57] *Dream and Reality*, p. 39.

ing concept of being is not applicable to God. God is; but He is not being in the sense of substance."[58] Nor even in the sense of Solovyov's *sushcheye*: "that which is."

With Kierkegaard and Kant, Berdyaev declared: "All the intellectual proofs of the existence of God are bankrupt." And he added (with Kierkegaard only!): "What is possible is an inward existential meeting with God."[59] In other words, an encounter with God as a person (*lichnost*).

Berdyaev's "personalism" involves the view that ultimate reality—"beyond [objectified] being"—is constituted by human persons, by the Divine Person, and by Christ, the Divine-Human Person, or God-Man (*Bogochelovek*).

Christianity extraordinarily exalts man in that it regards him as made in the image and likeness of God, recognizes a spiritual principle in him which raises him above the natural and social world. . . . Only on this Christian basis can a doctrine of personality (*lichnost*) be constructed and the personalist transvaluation of values be worked out.[60]

Persons are "in process," active, free, and creative. Or perhaps they simply *are* process, activity, freedom, creativity. As we have seen, freedom for Berdyaev is "meonic" not "ontal"; it requires, but cannot tolerate, objectification. When we press Berdyaev for a closer account of "freedom" or "spirit" he tends to fall into silence or into metaphor.

The silence suggests that not only Berdyaev's theology but also his general theory of persons and his philosophical anthropology are negative or "apophatic." The metaphor is sometimes vivid but seldom clarifying, as when Berdyaev declares that

[58] *Slavery and Freedom*, p. 75.
[59] *Truth and Revelation*, trans. R. M. French (New York, 1953), p. 95.
[60] *Slavery and Freedom*, p. 28.

"the nature of spirit is Heraclitean and not Parmenidean. Spirit is fire and energy."[61]

Shestov, in a late letter to Father Serge Bulgakov, declared his "great affection and respect for N. A. [Berdyaev]" but he added that Berdyaev's "leaning toward Athens" had always been a source of friction between them. Shestov was unhappy about Berdyaev's refusal to admit that the "tree of 'knowledge' is a threat to what is most precious to the living human being" and he was disturbed by Berdyaev's attempt to "reconcile" speculative and existential philosophy.[62] Shestov charged that, like Fichte, Berdyaev found the meaning of Christianity in John 1:1: "In the beginning was the Word (*Logos*)." "You deify ideas," Shestov complained, "and I cannot endure the deification of ideas."[63]

As Shestov pointed out, Berdyaev—in contrast to Dostoyevski, Kierkegaard, and Nietzsche (and, we might add, Shestov himself)—did not linger over religious and philosophical questions but hurried on to the answers, which seemed "to come to him of themselves." His writing is self-assured, even didactic, rather than experimental or questioning.[64] But Shestov generously added that Berdyaev was one of "the most humane philosophers," in the line of "that greatest of Russian human beings, Pushkin."[65] Berdyaev, we should note, reciprocated this

[61] *Freedom and the Spirit,* trans. Oliver F. Clarke (London, 1935), p. 15.

[62] Boulon-sur-Seine, October 26, 1938, in *Mosty,* 8 (1961):260. See also "N. Berdyayev," p. 226.

[63] Shestov to Berdyaev, Paris, 1923, in *Mosty,* 8 (1961):256.

[64] "N. Berdyayev," p. 203.

[65] An early critic, noting the "experimental" and questioning character of Shestov's writing, remarked that each of his books—like each of Nietzsche's—was *"ein Buch für Alle und Keinen"*: for "all" in the questions it posed, for "none" in the answers it gave (Ivanov-Razumnik, O

compliment, emphasizing the "humaneness" of Shestov as man and thinker.

Berdyaev admitted, in a letter to Shestov, that he had indeed written dogmatically and that he had not "revealed himself" because he was "closed in upon himself and probably too proud by nature." But he added that his was a genuine "tragedy of faith," emphasizing that "the whole of our [human] life is tragic, as is the whole of history."[66]

As early as 1905 Berdyaev had expressed his agreement with Shestov's view that the experience of tragedy is the foundation of ethics. "Only one who has taken tragedy into account can construct an ethics"; and therefore Nietzsche is a more profound ethicist than Kant.[67]

For all its intellectual penetration and rhetorical sparkle, Berdyaev's religious thought seems strangely limited and unsatis-factory. Perhaps even here he is too much the romantic and the aristocrat, preoccupied with his own feelings and responses, hypnotized by the depth of his own subjectivity, scornful and intolerant toward whatever he considered uncreative, unfree, "objectified." Unlike Shestov, Berdyaev did write a series of "fragments of a great confession." This confession, however, involves considerable "self-stylization" if not outright intellectual posturing.[68]

---

smysle zhizni: Fyodor Sologub, Leonid Andreyev, Lev Shestov [On the Meaning of Life: Fyodor Sologub, Leonid Andreyev, Leon Shestov] [St. Petersburg, 1908], pp. 162 f).

[66] Berlin, 1924, in Mosty, 8 (1961): 257 f.

[67] "Tragediya i obydennost" [Tragedy and Everydayness], Voprosy Zhizni, no. 3 (1905), pp. 282 f.

[68] See V. V. Zenkovsky, A History of Russian Philosophy, trans. George L. Kline (London: Routledge and Kegan Paul; New York: Columbia University Press, 1953), 2:763.

The contrast with Shestov is clear. There is not the least hint in Shestov's writings of "self-stylization" or posturing. Shestov strikes one as utterly honest and serious, single-mindedly engaged in a single battle: the battle against rational necessity and "self-evident truth" in the name of the values of human existence.[69] This may be just another way of saying that Shestov, although no less deeply religious than Berdyaev, was more profoundly a moralist.

[69] Shestov "combines elegance and power of expression with a rigor and purity of verbal form. The result is an irresistible impression of authenticity and honesty" (Zenkovsky, A History of Russian Philosophy, 2:781).

4

THE "GOD-BUILDERS":
GORKY AND LUNACHARSKI

The secular pseudo-religion of "God-building" (*bogostroitel-stvo*)[1] that flourished in the left wing of the Bolshevik faction of the Russian Social-Democratic (i.e., Marxist) Party during the decade after 1903 had at least three historical roots: (1) nineteenth-century Russian radicalism, (2) Feuerbach's left-Hegelian conversion of theology into philosophical anthropology, and (3) the Nietzschean doctrine of the "overman."

1. The tradition of nineteenth-century Russian radicalism is exemplified by Bazarov in Turgenev's novel *Fathers and Sons*. In opposition to their pious and aesthetically sensitive "fathers," who held that the world was essentially a "temple"—that is, a house of God and a place of beauty—the sons declared boldly: "The world is not a temple but a workshop" (*Mir ne khram, a masterskaya*). They meant, of course, not only, or even primarily, a factory for the production of gadgets but a laboratory

[1] The Russian word *bogostroitelstvo*, apparently coined by Gorky in 1908, is usually written with a small b. I have capitalized the English equivalent, 'God-building,' because it is not "a god" or "the gods" but God that is the object of this historical creation. The term *stroitelstvo*, of course, is regularly applied in Soviet parlance to the "building of socialism" (*stroitelstvo sotsializma*).

for the production of a biologically, psychologically, and socially perfected breed of men. They saw human history as a workshop in which an ideal man and an ideal society were to be forged.

To this tradition the "God-builders" of the early twentieth century added the claim that the ideal mankind of the future, vastly surpassing the frail, fragmented men of the present in power, creativity, and "beauty," will be truly divine. It will be supra-individual and "immortal," a source both of inspiration and consolation to impotent and perishing individuals. Why should it not be called "God"? Why not openly admit that the creation of an ideal mankind is "theogonic," that the building of the perfected human culture of the future is a "building of God"?

Bazarov's formula is then modified to read: The world is not *now* a temple; it is a workshop in which men labor *to* make the world holy, to transform it into an authentic temple. When mankind finally becomes godlike the world will finally be—in truth, not in illusion—a temple, a place of worship and reverence, and the repository for a new and lofty "socialist art."[2]

2. The second strand in the ideological fabric of *bogostroitelstvo* is Hegel's philosophy, as interpreted and developed in a one-sided way by the German "young Hegelians," especially Feuerbach. I cannot at this point enter into the complexities of Hegel's position; I limit myself to two remarks, neglecting technical detail.[3]

a. For Hegel, although speculative philosophy and revealed religion have the same object—namely, God or the "Absolute"

---

[2] The conception of a wholly new "socialist" or proletarian" culture (*proletkult*), unconnected to the "feudal" and "bourgeois" culture of the past, was developed during the early Soviet period by A. A. Bogdanov, with Lunacharski's strong support. It was soon officially repudiated.

[3] I shall say something further about Hegel's treatment of religion in chapter 5 (pp. 127–30).

—religious apprehension of this object is symbolic and defective whereas philosophical apprehension is conceptual and adequate.

b. Hegel's central category of spirit (*Geist*) is open to conflicting interpretations but a plausible interpretation makes Hegel either a pantheist or a philosophical humanist. What Hegel in the *Encyclopedia* and later works (but not in the *Phenomenology*) calls "Absolute Spirit" is—in this interpretation—not a transcendent but an immanent spiritual reality. And it is immanent in *human* history. This is part of what Hegel meant by calling the political state *der Gang Gottes in der Welt*—"God's march (or progress) in the world."

Feuerbach's reduction of theology to anthropology—that is, his transformation of the philosophical study of God into a philosophical study of man—grew directly out of this humanist reading of Hegel. For Feuerbach, God is "in process, in genesis, in travail." But Feuerbach insisted that what men call God is "nothing more than mankind comprehended in the totality of its history." Feuerbach's historical and psychological claim—that men have always in fact worshiped ideal mankind, projecting their own image into the cosmos, but have misidentified the object of their worship—is not essential to the "God-builders." Their primary emphasis is directed toward the *future*. They offer not so much an interpretation of the history of positive religions as a program for a new, purified "humanistic" religion.

"God-building," however, is unlike other humanistic religions or pseudo-religions, such as "Ethical Culture" and "Humanism," which consider human ideals and values to be worthy of reverence and piety here and now. There is a strong Kantian influence in "Ethical Culture," both in doctrine and in the historical filiation from German neo-Kantianism. For Kant, every man is an end in himself (*Selbstzweck*), of inviolable dignity.

But in "Ethical Culture" the Kantian position is truncated—by a rejection or simple ignoring of Kant's doctrine of the non-empirical, noumenal self and the realm of ends. The ethical culturist's "reverence for man" remains ungrounded.

The "God-builders" impatiently repudiated the Kantian ethic and philosophical anthropology as an expression of "petit bourgeois individualism." As Marxists they had little confidence in the values of the present generation of men, warped as it was by centuries of exploitation. Gorky and Lunacharski preached not the ideal *in* man, with the ethical culturists and humanists, or the ideal *above* man, with the theists, but the ideal *ahead* of man in history. Their piety and reverence was directed in anticipation toward a perfected *future* mankind, and by "future" they meant not so much five or fifty years hence as five hundred or twenty-five hundred years hence.

3. This historical and future-oriented "religious humanism" was powerfully inspired by Nietzsche. It is significant that the two major spokesmen for the "God-builders," Gorky and Lunacharski, as well as its two minor spokesmen, Bogdanov and V. A. Bazarov (whose real name was Rudnev), were specifically influenced by Nietzsche. Indeed, all of them may properly be called Nietzschean Marxists with respect to their ethics, social philosophy, and general theory of man.[4]

Nietzsche's theme of *futurity* is not to be found in Hegel and is only dimly implicit in Feuerbach. The idea of man's

[4] I have discussed the ethics and social philosophy of the "Nietzschean Marxists," Lunacharski, Volski, Bazarov, and Bogdanov, in "Changing Attitudes toward the Individual," in *The Transformation of Russian Society*, ed. C. E. Black (Cambridge, Mass.: Harvard University Press, 1960), esp. pp. 618–23; in "Theoretische Ethik im russischen Frühmarxismus," *Forschungen zur osteuropäischen Geschichte*, 9 (1963): esp. pp. 271 and 275–79; and in greater detail in " 'Nietzschean Marxism' in Russia," *The Boston College Studies in Philosophy*, vol. 2 (1968).

historical self-transcendence is built into Nietzsche's key term, *Übermensch*; the "overmen" will stand above and beyond the mere men who have lived in the past and who live today. Man, as Nietzsche put it, is something to be overcome. At best he is a bridge leading to the perfected *Übermensch*, whose free creativity, power, and passion will make the best creative efforts of historical men look awkward, weak, and foolish. "God is dead," Nietzsche proclaimed, but he added that man, though apelike, lives, and that the few "free spirits" in the present generation are building a bridge toward the godlike race of the future, toward the *Übermenschen*, toward trans-historical *Übermenschheit*.[5] This notion of an over-mankind or superhumanity was fully assimilated by the Russian "God-builders."

As I suggested in chapter 2, Nietzsche and Marx, despite their differences, share a post-Hegelian "culture-historical" orientation.[6] Nietzsche stands much closer to Hegel and Marx than to the existentialists. He does not value existential subjectivity or inwardness, as does Kierkegaard for example. He values cultural creativity; the individual is a means for enriching a cumulative culture in process of becoming.

[5] The expression "God is dead" or "God has died" (*dass Gott gestorben ist*) was used by Hegel in 1807 (cf. *Phänomenologie des Geistes*, Hoffmeister ed. [Leipzig, 1949], p. 532, and *Phenomonenology of Mind*, trans. J. B. Baillie [London and New York, 1931], p. 753). Hegel's phrase echoes a German hymn by Johannes Rist, which includes the lines: "*grosse Not/ dass Gott ist tot.*" In the hymn, of course, as in Hegel's text, the "death of God" refers not to the erosion of religious belief but to the Passion of Christ.

[6] Pp. 62–63. As early as 1841, in the preface to his doctoral dissertation, Marx quoted with warm approval the statement of the Aeschylean Prometheus: "I am the enemy of all the gods," adding that "philosophy" shared the Promethean hatred of "all heavenly and earthly gods which do not recognize human self-consciousness as the supreme deity. None shall stand beside it." *Marx-Engels Historisch-Kritische Gesamtausgabe* [Frankfurt, 1927], I, 1/1, p. 10.)

Nietzsche glorifies individuals as *creators* because he very sensibly doubts the creative power of committees or collectivities. He does not, however, value individuals as individuals. In Nietzsche's eyes the mystic, the sheer Aristotelian beholder, the poet who fails or refuses to publish his poems, and the artist who hides or destroys his works—whatever the depth and intensity of their subjective experience—are without value. In a word, Nietzsche does not recognize individual or personal but only cultural and social values. And culture, for him, is cumulative and historical.

In Nietzsche's view every society is anti-democratic, made up of the creative few and the uncreative many. But there is a kind of historical "democracy" that is made up of the great shapers and reshapers of cultural values from all societies. The few geniuses speak to each other, in Nietzsche's metaphor, from their lonely mountain heights across the wastelands of historical mediocrity. But as time goes on there will be more and more such geniuses, and they will be essentially equal in creative power, although of course those who come later will profit from what their predecessors have created.

The culture of the future, with a dozen or even a hundred creative giants in every generation equal to or greater than Rembrandt, Shakespeare, and Beethoven, will be far richer than anything we have known or can imagine. Such a culture, for Nietzsche, may well be called "godlike" or "divine" (*göttlich*). Its builders are, in a clear sense, "God-builders." Indeed, in *Beyond Good and Evil* Nietzsche had asserted, with evident satisfaction, that in contemporary Europe religious feeling was growing stronger while at the same time it was rejecting theism.[7]

This was precisely what the Russian "God-builders" a quarter

[7] *Beyond Good and Evil*, trans. Walter Kaufmann (New York: Vintage Books, 1966), sec. 53, p. 66.

108

of a century later believed; and they rejoiced in the fact. Let me turn now to the details of their doctrine.

I

Gorky, né Aleksei Maksimovich Peshkov, took the name Maxim Gorky—"Maxim the Bitter"—when, as a young writer in the 1890's, he found *la vita russa* anything but *dolce*.[8] He was born in 1868, just two years after Shestov, in the city of Nizhni Novgorod, since renamed Gorki. He had a difficult childhood, and began to work full time at the age of eight; he was sent out "into the world" at the age of nine. He traveled widely in Russia and worked at a variety of jobs, most of them unskilled. Once, when down and out, he tried to commit suicide.

Gorky had only a few months of formal education. His one attempt to enter the university (at Kazan) was abortive but it brought him into contact with radical student circles. By 1900 he had become a Marxist and had joined the party. In 1901 and again in 1905 he was arrested and imprisoned.

Gorky's first short stories were published in 1892. His neo-romantic glorification of wild, free gypsies and hoboes—non-conformists who lived on the outskirts of Russian society—had an immediate appeal. His literary success was enormous. He diverted the bulk of his considerable income from royalties into the Boshevik Party treasury, especially just before and after 1905.

Gorky's close contact with Lunacharski dates from 1909–11, when they collaborated in running a Bolshevik party school of Nietzschean leanings, first on Capri, where Gorky had settled in 1906, then at Bologna. Gorky returned to Russia under the amnesty of 1913. The Bolshevik revolution at first roused his

[8] His father's name, of course, was Maxim (Maksim) because his own patronymic was Maksimovich, that is, "son of Maxim."

enthusiasm but soon repelled him by its excesses and cruelties. He left the Soviet Union in 1921 and returned to Capri, ostensibly for reasons of health but in fact at Lenin's request. He visited the Soviet Union briefly in 1928 and returned to stay in 1933, on the occasion of his sixty-fifth birthday.

Gorky died suddenly in 1936 while undergoing medical treatment. Yagoda, the head of Stalin's secret police, confessed two years later (at the Moscow purge trials) that as part of a general Trotskyite plot against Soviet culture and the Stalinist regime he had ordered Gorky's doctors to poison him. However, many defendants at the Moscow trials confessed to things they could not possibly have done, and we may never know whether Yagoda actually had Gorky killed, nor on whose orders.

In general, Gorky's defense of the religion of "God-building" was literary and rhetorical rather than philosophical and critical. He *celebrated* the "building of God" and left to others, mainly Lunacharski, the theoretical elaboration of the doctrine. However, he provided the terminology that gave the movement a currency and notoriety it would probably not otherwise have had.

Gorky coined the terms and concepts "God-building" and "God-builder" (*bogostroitelstvo* and *bogostroitel*) in deliberate contrast to the terms and concepts "God-seeking" and "God-seeker" (*bogoiskatelstvo* and *bogoiskatel*), which were in general use in Russia from about 1903 on. The latter terms characterized religious thinkers who sought a "new religious consciousness," including not only Shestov and Berdyaev (whom we considered in chapter 3) but also such thinkers as S. N. Bulgakov, S. L. Frank, and Dimitri Merezhkovski.

In 1907 a certain Father Charpin conducted a kind of international Gallup poll on religious questions for the Paris journal *Mercure de France*. Among the respondents were Gorky and

Plekhanov. (Lunacharski had written about the socialist "religion of mankind" in 1905 but was not invited to respond to the enquête.) Gorky's response contains his major themes. "Religious feeling, as I understand the term," he said, "should exist, develop, and make man perfect." Gorky speaks of man's "imperious and proud desire to rival, in his creations, the generations of the past, and to create examples worthy of being followed by the generations of the future."[9]

In his response Gorky implicitly distinguished between two different objects of reverence and worship, and Lunacharski, commenting on Gorky's statement, made the distinction explicit: the natural universe and mankind as a whole, past, present, and especially future.[10] These two objects represent (1) the "cosmic" and (2) the "humanistic" or "anthropological" element of the new religious faith. The first is made up of what Gorky called the "joyous and proud sense of . . . a harmonious bond uniting man and the universe" and an "astonishment" at the "wise harmony that exists between man's spirit or mind (esprit) and that of the universe as a whole." The second comprises a sense of the "active bond" that unites past, present, and future generations, "faith in [man's] own powers," and "hope for his victory."[11]

As we shall see, Lunacharski denied the religious relevance of Gorky's "cosmic" element, but Gorky persisted in celebrating not only man-in-history but man-in-nature as well. He

[9] See "La question religieuse. Enquête internationale," Mercure de France, vols. 66–68 (1907); Gorky's response is in 66:592–95. In contrast to Gorky, Plekhanov asserted that the "religious idea" would disappear and that "religious feeling" would vanish along with it (Mercure de France, 66 [1907]:619).

[10] A. V. Lunacharski, "Budushcheye religii" [The Future of Religion], Obrazovaniye, no. 11 (1907), p. 31.

[11] "La question religieuse," 66:593–94.

referred to a lofty mountain peak in the Caucasus as a "touch-stone of man," which makes weak spirits "tremble before the power of the earth" but causes the strong to feel "proud and exalted."

Gorky's celebration of the "building of God" begins with a hymn to man. In his play *The Lower Depths* (1902) he used a phrase his Soviet admirers have made into a mandatory slogan: "*Chelovek! Eto zvuchit . . . gordo*" ("Man! That [word] has a . . . proud ring to it").[12] In another early play, *Children of the Sun* (1905), man is described as "the most brilliant, most beautiful phenomenon on earth."[13]

But man, for Gorky as for Nietzsche, is in the process of being evolved; and man's historical past has been marred by class division and exploitation. In the beginning, presumably during the period Engels had characterized as "primitive communism," God came into being "when men with one accord (*yedinodushno*) created him from the matter of their thought, in order to light up the darkness of [their] existence. But when the people was split into slaves and masters . . ., God died, God sank into decay."[14]

Gorky depicts the long period of historical slavery and serfdom as godless. Slaves, he insists, never had and "never will have a God, for God arises in the flame of the sweet conscious-

---

[12] *Na dne*, Act IV, in *Sochineniya* (Moscow, 1950), 6:170.

[13] *Deti solntsa*, Act I, in *Sochineniya*, 6:291.

[14] *Ispoved* [A Confession] (1908), in *Sochineniya*, 8:350 f. It was in this long short story that Gorky first used the terms *bogostroitelstvo* and *bogostroitel*. I have capitalized the word 'God' in this and other quotations from Gorky although his Soviet editors, here as elsewhere, write *Bog* with a small *b*. This orthographic atheism, which has been mandatory since 1918, has been applied by Soviet publishers not only to the pre-revolutionary works of Gorky but also to the Soviet reprintings of the works of such devout eighteenth- and nineteenth-century Russian writers and thinkers as Skovoroda, Dostoyevski, and Tolstoy. (There were occasional exceptions in the 1930's, including a volume of Tolstoy's complete works that

ness of the spiritual kinship of each with all. Temples are built
not from scraps and fragments but from strong, whole stones."[15]
In other words, the enterprise of "God-building" presupposes
a harmonious and cohesive social group—if not a solidary
society at least a solidary class.

In one place Gorky suggests that the working class is a natural
"God-builder"—whether in present class society or future classless society—while the ruling class is naturally hostile to the
enterprise of "God-building." "Mankind is divided into two
classes: the first is the eternal God-builder; the second is dominated by an overpowering desire to master the first. . . ." Typically, Gorky speaks neither of classes nor societies but simply
of "the people" (narod), meaning the mass of ordinary men.
He calls the people "omnipotent" (vsesilny) and "immortal"
(bessmertny).[16]

"The builder of God," Gorky writes, "is the people [he uses
the "caressing" diminutive form, narodushko]. . . . Thou art
God, perform miracles! The people is immortal. . . . It is the
father of all gods past and future."[17] The "God-builders,"
Gorky adds, who are "alive and immortal," now "secretly and
diligently are building a new God." In the end, Gorky assures
us, the people, will find "the one true path to a universal fusion
(sliyaniye), for the sake of the great cause or task (delo), the
cause of universal God-building."[18]

---

was published in 1933, in which Bog appeared regularly with a capital letter,
but a Pushkin edition was actually recalled by the Soviet publishers because
of un-atheistic capitalization!) The works of such religious thinkers as
Leontyev, Rozanov, Shestov, and Berdyaev have never been reprinted in the
Soviet Union.

[15] Sochineniya, 8: 352.
[16] Ibid., p. 378.
[17] Perhaps an echo of the Homeric Zeus, "father of men and gods"
(pater andrōn te theōn te)?
[18] Sochineniya, 8:331, 378.

The faith of the "God-builders" springs not from weakness but from strength, from an overflow of vital energies. The faith of a solidary community is creative, even thaumaturgic. A "humanistic miracle" climaxes Gorky's story *A Confession:* the common people, united in spirit, bend their collective will to healing a paralyzed girl.

As the rain soaks the earth with its living moisture, so the people filled the girl's dessicated body with their own strength. . . . We seized the girl, lifted her up, and set her on the ground; we held her lightly, and she swayed down like an ear of grain in the wind. . . . She stopped, shook herself—and walked. . . . She stretched her hands out in front of her, resting them on air saturated with the strength of the people.[19]

The new religion, Gorky claims, will banish the fear of death that now "hangs over men like a black cloud, covering the earth with shadows."

We . . . children of the sun, born of the sun, the shining source of life, will conquer the dark fear of death. . . . The sun burns in our blood . . . ; it is an ocean of energy, of beauty, and of soul-intoxicating joy![20]

In the early (1904) prose poem *Chelovek* [Man], Gorky hinted at an eventual Promethean achievement of physical, or at least personal and non-spiritual, immortality. "Thought," he wrote, "enviously studies [death]—Thought, creative and brilliant, like the sun, filled with the insane audacity and proud consciousness of immortality." Gorky is "firmly convinced . . . of the immortality and eternal growth of the creativity of [thought]," and he adds: "I walk in the radiance of immortal thought." When "immortal thought" and feeling fuse into a

[19] *Ibid.,* pp. 376 f.
[20] *Deti solntsa,* Act II, in *Sochineniya,* 6:326.

114

single creative flame, "I will be like unto those gods which my Thought has created and continues to create."[21]

It remains unclear, despite—or perhaps because of—Gorky's impassioned but rather muddy rhetoric, just how the religion of "God-building" is to help men overcome the fear of death. Gorky tends to fall back on the familiar exhortation to lose oneself in a greater human whole. To forget oneself, Gorky writes, is to be aware that one is "a link in the exquisite and immense, unending chain" of historical mankind, what he elsewhere calls "the majestic, harmonious organism of humanity" that is "destined to know everything, to control creation." Eventually, Gorky insists, not only will men have a vivid sense of their connection with the past, man will have, "in equal measure, a clear conception of the influence of his mind and spirit (esprit) upon the future."[22] "In the [social] whole," Gorky admonishes, "you will find immortality, but in solitude—inevitable slavery and darkness, inconsolable sorrow and death."[23]

Gorky insists that the "fusion of human souls" in the historical collective is entirely different from the union or communion of a traditional believer with a transcendent God. In the first case there is "forgetfulness of the self"; in the second case there is "elimination or destruction of the self." This socialist-humanist "fusion of souls" will become possible only "on the morrow of the social revolution," when, according to Gorky, the "living religion of socialism" will replace the "worn-out religion of Christianity."

Rozanov, who as we have seen had his own critical reservations about nineteenth-century Christianity, expressed general

[21] In Sochineniya, 5:364, 367. I shall return to the theme of physical immortality in chapter 6 (pp. 165–67).
[22] "La question religieuse," 66:595.
[23] Ispoved, in Sochineniya, 8:352.

115

sympathy for Gorky's religion of "generation-after-generation—the people" (a pun in Russian: *Rod-na-rod—narod*), and added that this was "perhaps 'still a church' and certainly a Tower of Babel."[24]

Unfortunately, Lenin had quite different ideas about what should and would replace Christianity, and all other historical religions, on the morrow of the Russian "social revolution." However, I shall defer consideration of Lenin's critique of the Russian Marxist "God-builders" until we have examined Lunacharski's version of the new doctrine.

II

Anatoli Vasilyevich Lunacharski was born in Poltava in the Ukraine in 1875, seven years after Gorky and one year after Berdyaev, of cultured and well-to-do parents. His father, a government official, was said to have had "advanced opinions." As a fifteen-year-old student at the Kiev *gymnasium* Lunacharski became involved in revolutionary, and later specifically Marxist, circles. As a consequence he was formally disqualified from matriculating at any university in the Russian Empire; however, he attended lectures at the University of Kiev, and there he met Berdyaev.

At the age of seventeen Lunacharski went abroad; he spent two years in Zurich (1892–94) and two years in Paris (1894–96). In Zurich he heard the lectures of Richard Avenarius, the "empiriocritical" philosopher, and became a convert to neo-positivist "empiriocriticism." Lunacharski returned to Russia in

[24] Undated letter from Rozanov to Gorky, probably written between 1912 and 1914; published in *Beseda* (Berlin), no. 2 (1923), p. 412, and reprinted in V. V. Rozanov, *Izbrannoye* [Selected Works], ed. Yu. Ivask (New York, 1956), p. 192.

1897, and in 1899 was arrested and exiled to Vologda for a three-year period. His exile was shared by Berdyaev, who at that time was a convinced if somewhat unconventional Marxist.

A Bolshevik after 1903, Lunacharski was summoned to Geneva by Lenin in 1904 but he returned to Russia in October, 1905, in time to take part in the December uprising. In the sequel, Lunacharski was again arrested and briefly imprisoned. Abroad after 1907, Lunacharski, a leader of the left wing of the Bolshevik faction, was active (as we have seen) in the party schools on Capri and in Bologna (1909–11). He spent the war years in France and Switzerland.

After the February revolution Lunacharski, like Lenin, returned to Russia through Germany in a "sealed train." He was arrested after the July uprising but was released. He rejoined Lenin's wing of the Bolsheviks after October and was appointed the first People's Commissar for Education, a post he held until 1929, when Stalin reassigned him to the foreign service. In 1933 Lunacharski was named Soviet ambassador to Spain but he did not serve in that post. He became ill en route to Spain and died at Menton, on the French Riviera, in December, 1933.

Lunacharski developed his own doctrine of a socialistic "religion of mankind" as an explicit reaction against the superficial "enlightenmentism" of G. V. Plekhanov, who at the turn of the century was regarded as the leading philosopher of the Russian Marxist movement. Lunacharski considered Plekhanov a typical eighteenth-century *philosophe*, not only in his "materialist metaphysics" but also, and especially, in his attitude toward religion. For Plekhanov, religious doctrines were essentially superstitions, intellectual errors due to ignorance or the weight of tradition. Religious attitudes and feelings, according to

Plekhanov, will "wither away" along with religious doctrines.[25]

Lunacharski found this view false, narrow, "pre-Marxist," and even "pre-Feuerbachian." It failed to grasp the human heart of religion beneath the trappings of theology and liturgy. It failed to comprehend the momentous achievement of Feuerbach and Marx, who gave "human self-consciousness its final boost in becoming human religion."[26] Lunacharski placed Marx in the line of religious geniuses—with Isaiah, Christ, St. Paul, and Spinoza—who are "Judaism's precious gifts to mankind." He characterized Marx's "religious feeling" as a "warm sense of his kinship, his being a part of the infant God [i.e., historical mankind], and [as] an understanding of the value of individual life only as bound up with the grandiose sweep of collective life."[27]

In sharp opposition to Plekhanov, Lunacharski sees continuing vitality and relevance in religious feeling, conceived broadly as "a supreme ecstasy, an enthusiasm, in which the individual is dissolved and transcended, in which he enters into joyous communion with a higher principle."[28]

As early as 1904—four years before Gorky coined the term *bogostroitelstvo*—Lunacharski sketched the broad outlines of

[25] Plekhanov's views on religion will be examined in chapter 5. We may note here that he reciprocated Lunarcharski's scorn: he called him a "haystack" that had somehow managed to influence the "Mt. Blanc" of Gorky's genius. He mockingly labeled Lunacharski a "God-composer" (*bogosochinitel*) and his doctrine a "God-composing" or "God-spinning" (*bogosochinitelstvo*). See G. V. Plekhanov, *Sochineniya* (Moscow, 1926), 17:271 f, 266.

[26] "Budushcheye religii" [The Future of Religion], *Obrazovaniye*, no. 10 (1907), p. 14.

[27] *Religiya i sotsializm* [Religion and Socialism] (St. Petersburg, 1911), 2:228, 347.

[28] "Budushcheye religii, *Obrazovaniye*, no. 11 (1907), p. 30.

the "new religion" and made explicit reference to its "Promethean strivings."

> The faith of the active human being is a faith in future mankind; his religion is an aggregate of those feelings and thoughts which make him a co-participator in the life of mankind, a link in the chain which stretches toward the overman [*sverkhchelovek* = Nietzsche's *Übermensch*], toward a beautiful and powerful creature, a perfected organism. . . .[29]

In 1908 Lunacharski confidently announced that "in Russia and in the West a new religion is actually being elaborated."[30] This socialist, Marxist-based religion is essentially a theory, or system, of values (Lunacharski quoted with approval Höffding's general characterization of religion as concern for the fate of values). Every philosophy performs what Lunacharski calls a "religious" function insofar as it makes value judgments about the world and man's place in it. "To evaluate means to bring that which is valued into relation to our vital needs."[31] The "religion of socialism," like every religion, offers the consoling hope that life will vanquish evil and death.

Religion "testifies to the presence of evil in the world and seeks a victory over it." But, unlike traditional theisms, the religion of "God-building" lacks "even a trace of worship of anything non-human, even a trace of a 'guarantee' [of the victory of good over evil]."[32] Religion is "that mode of conceiving and feeling the world which provides a psychological resolution

---

[29] "Osnovy pozitivnoi estetiki" [Fundamentals of Positivist Aesthetics], in *Ocherki realisticheskovo mirovozzreniya* [Essays in a Realistic World View], ed. S. Dorovatovski and A. Charushnikov (St. Petersburg, 1904), p. 181.

[30] "Ateizm" [Atheism], in *Ocherki po filosofii marksizma* [Essays in the Philosophy of Marxism], (St. Petersburg, 1908), p. 164.

[31] "Budushcheye religii," *Obrazovaniye*, no. 10, p. 24.

[32] *Religiya i sotsializm*, 2:220, 347.

of the tension between the laws of life and the laws of nature." The "laws of life" are normative or prescriptive laws; they specify what *should* be the case. The "laws of nature" are factual or descriptive laws; they specify what *is*—and often should not be—the case. (The tension described by Lunacharski is reminiscent of that between the "ideal" and the "real" in human existence which John Dewey, in *A Common Faith*, proposed to call "God.") This tension will be resolved, Lunacharski assures us, through the Promethean project of subduing nature —by the application of man's "knowledge and labor, science and technology."[33]

This Promethean project alone, however, will not overcome the terror of death. "Longing lives in man," Lunacharski confesses, "and he who is unable to conceive the world religiously is doomed to pessimism, unless he be a simple Philistine. . . ."[34] Pessimism can be overcome by cultivating those "solemn, supraindividual feelings which raise man to the heights of enthusiasm and save him from death."[35] Such religious enthusiasm involves a deepened awareness of what Lunacharski calls "the universal connectedness of life, of the *all-life* (*vsezhizn*) which triumphs even in death."[36] There is an "unconscious" and traditional way of "conquering death," says Lunacharski— loosely paraphrasing Plato—namely, through sexual love and procreation. But there is a higher, "conscious" way: through love for the human species and human culture.

Human rationality may be either "small" or "large" (Lunacharski adapted this rather careless terminology from Nietzsche).

[33] "Budushcheye religii," *Obrazovaniye*, no. 10, pp. 21, 22 (italics removed).

[34] *Ibid.*, p. 21.

[35] "Budushcheye religii," *Obrazovaniye*, no. 11, p. 43.

[36] "Yeshcho o teatre i sotsializme" [Once More on the Theater and Socialism], in *Vershiny* (St. Petersburg, 1909), p. 213.

Corresponding to the "small rationality" is a narrow, "micro-psychic" individualism. Corresponding to the "large rationality," the reason of the species, is "macropsychic" individualism. The "we," says Lunacharski, is a

"greater I" [that] makes it possible to rejoice in victories that will be achieved a century after the death of the "little I," to live the life of generations long dead, which also were a part of the "we." . . . This is individualism, since the circumference of the "we" includes the "I"; the "I" . . . does not have to love anything external or alien to it; but it is macropsychic individualism—breadth of soul —as distinguished from egoism, however "rational," which remains a kind of micropsychism—a narrowness of soul.[37]

Only "macropsychic individualism," of course, is capable of vanquishing death—or rather the fear of death.

Although Lunacharski agreed with Gorky on the broad outlines of the new "religion of mankind," "religion of feeling," or "religion of socialism," he rejected the "cosmic" element of Gorky's doctrine (see pp. 111–12 above). Reverence and piety, Lunacharski argued, must involve not only wonder and awe, which we properly feel toward nature, but also gratitude, which we do not.

Nature—the "universal mother" or "all-mother (vsemater)— is indifferent to our joys and sorrows. She creates us without favor and destroys us without malice. In her presence we can feel awestruck or astonished, but hardly grateful. Gratitude is appropriate only toward mankind as a whole in its historical development. Religious feeling—as opposed to awe, admiration, or even love of nature—is either filial (directed toward past generations) or parental (directed toward future generations).

Lunacharski describes the religion of mankind as filled with

[37] "Voprosy morali i M. Meterlink" [Questions of Morality and M. Maeterlinck] (1904); reprinted in Lunacharski's Etyudy (Moscow, 1922), pp. 255 f.

drama and passion, having its own "saints and martyrs" and worthy to stand beside Roman Catholicism in the "universal arsenal of art and inspiration."[38] It fills men with a sense of "joyous union with the triumphant future of our species," a future that promises unheard-of cultural achievements. Lunacharski speaks with emotion of "the miracles of [human] culture in the year 3000."[39]

The mental powers of our "not-so-remote descendants," Lunacharski avers, "will exceed ours by as monstrous a margin as the brain-power of Faraday and Marconi exceeds the power of a protozoon's nerve cell." Sometimes Lunacharski puts his Promethean point in quasi-Christian language: When we know that man's thought "flies on the wings of electricity from one hemisphere to the other," he asks, "do we not feel how the [infant] God born between the ox and the donkey has grown strong?"[40]

Marxist socialism, because of its wholehearted involvement in building man's godlike future, Lunacharski insists, is "the most religious of all religions," and the true Marxist Socialist is "the most deeply religious of men."[41]

At least one Marxist Socialist remained unconvinced—and when Lenin spoke, even as early as 1909, the Bolshevik Central Committee paid attention. Late in 1909 this committee officially condemned the doctrine of "God-building," and Gorky and Lunacharski lapsed into silence on the subject of religion. Lunacharski publicly recanted in 1923 and rather ostentatiously

---

[38] *Kritika chistovo opyta . . . Avenariusa* [Avenarius' Critique of Pure Experience], ed. and introd. A. V. Lunacharski (Moscow, 1905), p. 154.

[39] "Yeshcho o teatre," in *Vershiny*, p. 212.

[40] *Religiya i sotsializm*, 1:48, 104.

[41] "Budushcheye religii," *Obrazovaniye*, no. 10, p. 23.

jumped onto the bandwagon of Leninist anti-religious militance. During the 1920's he took part in a series of public debates with Metropolitan Alexander Vvedenski, head of the so-called "Living Church," which was much closer to the regime than the Russian Orthodox church. Several of Lunacharski's speeches were published in 1926 under the title *Christianity or Communism?* His position in these debates and in other statements of the period was scarcely distinguishable from that of Lenin and Bakunin.

Lunacharski, for example, declared in 1923 that the final victory over theistic and supernaturalistic religion would come in the not-too-distant future. The proletariat "is throwing off religion like a dreadful deception . . . and is shattering the privileges of those classes which have an interest in keeping human consciousness in the ancient and rusty fetters of religion." The belief in personal immortality, Lunacharski added, is a "peasant belief" that no intelligent person can take seriously.[42]

Gorky, when challenged, merely restated in non-religious language what he had been trying to say in *A Confession* about the religion of "God-building."

I am an atheist. In *A Confession* I was attempting to show the ways in which a man may move from individualism to a collectivistic conception of the world. . . . The hero of *A Confession* understands by "God-building" the ordering of the people's existence in a collectivistic spirit, in the spirit of the union of all men on the path to a single goal—namely, the liberation of man from internal and external slavery.[43]

Lenin's attack on Gorky, in two long letters that were written in 1913 and are pedantically appended by Soviet editors as a

[42] *Nauka, Iskusstvo, Religiya* [Art, Science, Religion] (Moscow, 1923), pp. 37, 39, 14.

[43] In Gorky, *Sochineniya*, 8:504.

kind of ideological vaccine to all editions of *A Confession*, was typically vitriolic. Lenin had very few arguments against the new religion of "God-building" but he made it clear from the start that he detested it, chiefly because it was much more difficult to discredit than the plainer "old-time religions."

> The Catholic priest [Lenin declared] who seduces young girls (of whom I just now happened to read in a German newspaper) is far less dangerous . . . than a priest without a frock, a priest without a coarse religion, a democratic priest with ideas, who preaches the building and creating of god (*sozidaniye i sotvoreniye bozhenki*).[44]

Lenin denied that there is any essential difference between the theistic religion of the "God-seekers" and the "purified" humanistic religion of the "God-builders." In his own vulgar but vivid simile, they are as much alike as a blue devil and a yellow devil.

Such vulgarity permeates Lenin's statements on religion; he almost never used the ordinary Russian word *Bog* for 'God' but, instead, the familiar diminutive *bozhenka*, invariably written with a small *b*. The term may be used non-disparagingly, as in children's stories, but Lenin's systematic use of it was unmistakably disparaging in its intent and offensive in its effect.

Lenin's arguments, such as they are, boil down to three.

1. Man's worship of mankind is Philistine and narcissistic. It is typical of a class, the bourgeoisie, that is "desperate and exhausted," and that in its "self-contemplation and self-admiration" concentrates on "the dirtiest, stupidest, most grovelling features" of its own ego, features that are "deified by god-building."[45]

2. Gorky's "sugar-coating" or "gilding" of the idea of God

---

[44] Lenin to Gorky, November 13 or 14, 1913, in V. I. Lenin, *Sochineniya*, 5th ed. (Moscow, 1964), 48:227 (italics removed).
[45] *Loc. cit.*

is a gilding of the chains the ruling classes have fastened upon the "ignorant workers and peasants." Lenin admits that there was a time in history when the struggle of the proletariat took the form of a struggle of one religious idea against another, but that time, he insists, has long since passed. At the present time (1913), "every advocacy or justification of the idea of god, even the most subtle, the best-intentioned, is a justification of reaction." Lenin considered Gorky's conception of God to be "bourgeois" as well as "reactionary."[46]

3. Religious feelings do not, as Gorky claimed, strengthen social solidarity or reinforce the cohesiveness of the collective:

The idea of god has always deadened and dulled "social feelings" . . . and has always been an idea of slavery (the worst, hopeless kind of slavery). The idea of god has never "bound the individual to society," but has always bound the oppressed classes by a belief in the divinity of the oppressors.[47]

The violence of Lenin's response to the doctrine of "God-building" must have surprised Gorky and Lunacharski, both of them longtime friends and party comrades of Lenin. Of course, by 1913 they should have known that Lenin did not permit mere friendship to blunt the edge of his ideological hatchet. This had become evident in his attacks on Bogdanov, Bazarov, and Lunacharski in the ill-tempered and polemical book of 1909, *Materialism and Empiriocriticism*.

Although Lenin's "refutation" of the position of the "God-builders" was clumsy and primitive, he seems dimly to have grasped a pertinent truth; namely, that the utopianism and romanticism of both Gorky and Lunacharski would be difficult to reconcile with hard-headed social engineering. Lenin directed his criticism more explicitly and more fully at Gorky than at

[46] *Ibid.*, pp. 230, 231.
[47] *Ibid.*, p. 232 (italics removed).

Lunacharski, but it was the latter's ethical position—an "individualism," even if "macropsychic"—that offered the greater threat to Leninist collectivism. Gorky, despite his Nietzscheanism, remained essentially a collectivist.

The details of Lenin's view of religion will be considered in chapter 5. I want only to mention at this point that, despite the official repudiation of the religion of "God-building," elements of it persisted—and, I think, still persist in the pseudo-religious technological Prometheanism accepted by a fairly large group within the scientific and technical elite of Soviet society. But consideration of this topic must be deferred until the sixth and final chapter.

5

THE MARXIST CRITIQUE:
PLEKHANOV AND LENIN

I

In chapter 4, which was devoted to the "God-builders" among the early Russian Marxists, we had occasion to consider the impetus that Hegel's philosophy of religion, perhaps contrary to Hegel's intention, gave to the development of a humanistic and Promethean "religion of mankind." The chief difference between the early Hegel and the "God-builders," we saw, was the difference between the assertion that the divine is wholly immanent in human history and culture and the assertion that mankind, as creator of a deepening historical culture, is potentially—will be able to make itself—divine. In considering the Marxist critique of traditional religions as this critique was formulated by Plekhanov and Lenin, beginning in the 1890's, we must recur to Hegel's philosophy of religion. But in this context we are concerned with a rather different emphasis of Hegel's thought; namely, the view that religion is a transition form in the historical development of the human spirit.

Hegel was the first major European thinker to see religions—and religion—as historical phenomena, phenomena that arise, flourish, decay, and are superseded at specific times and in specific places. Hegel's view is entirely antithetical to that of the *philosophes* of the French enlightenment who had held that religious beliefs, being in essence errors and superstitions, would evaporate without a trace under the noonday sun of positive knowledge. For the "enlighteners," medieval Europe, dominated by a profoundly religious view of the world, was a "dark age," intellectually void, a total historical loss. For Hegel, in contrast, nothing human is wasted or lost. Each historical epoch or phase has its special and positive function and value; each is a partial, inadequate expression of a larger and more adequate truth. The "truth of the whole" is a synthesis that is forged out of the conflicting untruths of the subordinate historical *Momente*, or dialectical phases.

In his first major work, the *Phenomenology of the Spirit* (1807), Hegel traced the development of human religion through a series of historical representations or symbolizations of "Absolute Being," from least to most adequate. At the beginning of this series stand the "nature religions," which take one aspect of the natural world (e.g., in Zoroastrianism the light of the rising sun) and treat it as divine. Next come the religions that revere plants and animals (Hindu worship of the lotus, sacred cow, and sacred monkey; totemism; and the like). The religion of ancient Egypt is not a religion of mere nature but is not yet a religion of human art or culture. It stands at the intermediate stage of "artifice" or "artifact" where natural elements are combined into an almost crystalline product that lacks the organic unity of a created work of art. In the Egyptian religion, in Hegel's view, the monstrous artifact of the man-eagle or the lion-woman (i.e., the sphinx) is taken as divine.

Artistic and cultural creativity, as contrasted with mere artifice, enters history at the higher stage of Greek religion. We cannot follow the complex details of Hegel's treatment of Greek religion here; the important point for our purposes is that Christianity—as a religion of revelation, of symbolic disclosure of the truth about "Absolute Being"—is a dialectical completion and transcendence of the lower forms of religion: the religion of nature, the religion of artifice and artifact, and the religion of art and culture.[1] But for Hegel, even Christianity is not the final truth.

As Hegel sees the relationship between art, religion, and philosophy, art as a "sensuous representation" (*Vorstellung*) gives way—dialectically and historically—to religion as a "represented concept" (*vorgestellter Begriff*), which in turn gives way to philosophy, or "absolute knowledge," as an adequate conceptualization (*Begriff*)—purged of every symbolic and sensuous element—of "Absolute Being." Thus, in Hegel's view, Christianity, although it is the highest form of historical religion—or the highest historical form of religion—is *not* the most adequate mode of grasping the object of all religions, namely, God or the "Absolute." As Kierkegaard was to put it (perhaps a bit unfairly), Hegel viewed Christianity as the tentative and defective first edition of a book of which Hegelian speculative philosophy was the revised and authoritative second edition!

Setting aside the technical details of Hegel's position, we may say that Hegel asserted, and tried to give a rational account of, the defective and transitional character of all positive or historical religions, Christianity included. Religion for him is a spiritual bridge, a bridge that leads to the "absolute knowledge" of speculative philosophy. And speculative philosophy burns

[1] For helpful commentaries on the pre-Christian stages of religion in Hegel's *Phenomenology*, see Jacob Loewenberg, *Hegel's* Phenomenology: Dialogues on the Life of Mind (La Salle, Ill.: Open Court, 1965), pp. 292–333, and Jean Hyppolite, *Genèse et structure de la Phénoménologie de l'Esprit de Hegel* (Paris, 1946), pp. 511–37.

its spiritual bridges behind it, leaving only the ashes of its *aufgehobene Momente*—that is, of the inferior dialectical phases that, as "absolute knowledge," it has canceled, preserved, and raised to a higher level. Religion is present in philosophy only as an *aufgehobenes Moment*.

Marx took over Hegel's position and extended it in a one-sided and single-minded way. He held, with Hegel, that religion is a historically conditioned and transitional phenomenon. Whereas Hegel had said that religion points to a total truth above and beyond its own defective or partial truth, Marx, however, preferred to say that religion, as total untruth, was fated to give way to a total, and totally non-religious, truth.

This Marxist "truth beyond religion" is twofold. On the one hand, religious *doctrine* is to be superseded by "science"—not in the broad and inclusive sense of Hegel's *Wissenschaft* but in the narrower sense of the empirical sciences: physics, astronomy, chemistry, biochemistry, physiology, psychology, and perhaps "scientific" philosophy. (Marx is ambiguous on this last point, but Engels often preached a positivistic dissolution of philosophy into the special sciences. Like Plekhanov later, Engels had a much more robust faith than Marx in the automatic supersession of religion by advancing science.)

On the other hand, religious *attitudes* and *values* and religiously based *morality* are to be superseded by secular attitudes and values and by "socialist morality." According to Marx and the Marxists, the new attitudes and values and the new morality in the period *before* the social revolution provide a support for the class struggle of the proletariat. In the period *after* the revolution, when the class war has been won, the new attitudes and values and the new morality will support the Promethean struggle of a liberated mankind against the hostile forces of non-human nature.

In both cases—with respect to doctrine and also with respect to attitudes, values, and conduct—religion is viewed by Marx and the Marxists as a historically transient phenomenon, inextricably bound up with the socio-economic system of capitalist (and pre-capitalist) exploitation, and doomed to "wither away" with the approach to a non-exploitative, classless socio-economic system.

As early as 1843 Marx declared that "the criticism of religion is the premise of all [other] criticism" (he meant primarily social and political criticism). And he added:

Man, who has found only the reflection (Widerschein) of himself in the fantastic reality of heaven where he sought a supernatural being (Übermensch), will no longer be inclined to find the semblance (Schein) of himself, only the non-human being (Unmensch), where he seeks and must seek his own reality.[2]

This is somewhat less than crystal clear, but I take Marx to be saying, with Feuerbach and Bakunin (although, of course, long before Bakunin had gotten around to saying it), that when men realize that the God of traditional religions is only an idealized projection of themselves they will, at the same time, come to appreciate their own power and dignity, their own true humanity, as active transformers of this world.

Marx spells this point out somewhat more fully in the sequel.

The basis of irreligious criticism is this: Man makes religion, religion does not make man. And indeed religion is the [defective] self-

[2] Karl Marx, "Zur Kritik der Hegelschen Rechtsphilosophie. Einleitung," in Marx-Engels Historisch-Kritische Gesamtausgabe (MEGA) (Frankfurt, 1927), I/1, p. 607. A convenient English translation is "Toward the Critique of Hegel's Philosophy of Law: Introduction," in Writings of the Young Marx on Philosophy and Society, ed. and trans. Loyd D. Easton and Kurt H. Guddat (New York: Doubleday Anchor Books, 1967), pp. 249–250.

consciousness and self-regard of man who has either not yet found or has already lost himself.[3]

Religious consciousness, according to Marx, is an inverted or perverted consciousness that has been produced by the inverted or perverted social world of feudalism and capitalism. Of course, in one sense this "inverted or perverted consciousness" is a "true" consciousness, even though it is objectively false and thus "unscientific"—in the sense, namely, in which it adequately and accurately reflects an "inverted and perverted" socio-economic system.[4]

Such a position is a step backward from Hegel, via Feuerbachian vulgarization, into the eighteenth century. In this philosophical retreat both Plekhanov and Lenin abjectly followed their master. Marx, like Feuerbach, sees religion as the imaginary realization or actualization (*Verwirklichung*) of a human nature that, because of socio-economic alienation and exploitation, has no true reality or actuality (*Wirklichkeit*). "The struggle against religion," he concludes, "is therefore indirectly (*mittelbar*) the struggle against that [socio-economic] world whose spiritual aroma is religion."[5] In a word, anti-religion is a part of the general class struggle, a point Lenin in due season was to insist upon.

Waxing even more rhetorical, Marx declared, in a celebrated passage:

Religion is the sigh of the oppressed creature. . . . It is the *opium* of the people.

[3] MEGA, I/1, 607; "Critique of Hegel's Philosophy of Law," p. 250.

[4] See Nicholas Lobkowicz, "Karl Marx's Attitude toward Religion," *Review of Politics*, 26 (1964): p. 321. This thoughtful and perceptive article has been reprinted as Chap. 14 of *Marx and the Western World*, ed. Nicholas Lobkowicz (London and Notre Dame, Ind.: Notre Dame University Press, 1967), pp. 303–35.

[5] "Zur Kritik," in MEGA, p. 607; and "Critique of Hegel's Philosophy of Law," p. 250 (italics removed).

The abolition (*Aufhebung*) of religion as people's *illusory* happiness is the demand for their *real* happiness. . . . The criticism of religion is thus in embryo a criticism of the vale of tears whose halo (*Heiligenschein*) is religion.

Criticism has plucked imaginary flowers from the chain [that binds man], not so that man will wear the chain that is without fantasy or consolation but so that he will throw it off and pluck the living flower.

Shifting to an astronomical metaphor, Marx added:

The criticism of religion disillusions man . . . so that he revolves around himself and thus around his true sun. Religion is only the illusory sun that revolves around man so long as he does not revolve about himself.[6]

Philosophy, according to Marx, has the task of following up the unmasking of religious justification and sanctification of socio-economic alienation with the more fundamental unmasking of the "unholy" self-alienation of man in exploitative society. "The criticism of heaven turns into the criticism of the earth, the criticism of religion into the criticism of law (*Recht*), and the criticism of theology into the criticism of politics."[7]

We shall pursue the above points in their Leninist formulation at the end of the present chapter. First, a word or two about the "withering away" of religion. This metaphorical notion of "withering away" or "dying out" (in Marx's and Engels' German, *Absterben*; in Plekhanov's and Lenin's Russian, *otmiraniye*) presupposes the conceptual model of society as a plant-like organism that has leaves as well as roots. The root of the social plant is the economic "base"; the foliage is the political and ideological "superstructure." The social revolution

---

[6] "Zur Kritik," pp. 607, 608; "Critique of Hegel's Philosophy of Law," p. 250 (italics partially removed).

[7] "Zur Kritik," p. 608; "Critique of Hegel's Philosophy of Law," p. 251 (italics removed).

is intended to cut the exploitative root of capitalist society, whereupon its ideological foliage, specifically including religious beliefs and attitudes, will inevitably wither and die.[8]

"Withering away" for a Marxist really means "self-elimination" or "self-liquidation," that is, "elimination by the objective movement of history." The *Absterbenstheorie* is a deterministic doctrine. Whether the social revolution itself, with its accompanying abolition of private ownership of the means of production is or is not historically determined, the impact upon the ideological "superstructure" of these upheavals in the economic "base" must be direct and automatic. Here, as elsewhere, Lenin sharply modified Marx's determinism.

Just as Lenin's militant call to action in *What Is to Be Done?* (1902) tacitly undercut historical determinism, his forthright attack on religion constituted an implicit recognition that religion is *not* historically self-liquidating—or at least does not disappear quickly or completely enough to satisfy a Marxist-Leninist—and hence must be actively liquidated by the collective efforts of dedicated men who are afire with the passion not of "God-building" but of "God-unbuilding"—intent upon suppressing every sign and symbol of divine transcendence.

II

The two principal theorists of anti-religion in early Russian Marxism, Plekhanov and Lenin, represent, respectively, the two aspects of the Marxist critique of religion we referred to earlier.

[8] For further discussion of the Marxist conception of the withering away of ideologies and institutions, see my essay, "The Withering Away of the State: Philosophy and Practice," in *The Future of Communist Society*, ed. Walter Laqueur and Leopold Labedz (London and New York: Frederick Praeger, 1962), pp. 63–71.

For Plekhanov, religion is "bad" science, "pseudo-science," that inevitably will give way to "good"—wholly secular—science. For Lenin, religion in the twentieth century is capitalist "opium," an arm of bourgeois politics that will give way, once exploitation is abolished, to the values and attitudes of socialist collectivism.

To put the point differently: Plekhanov saw religion as a pure, almost innocent, superstition; Lenin saw religion as a superstition with a sinister social purpose. Like Bakunin, Lenin believed that a man's effectiveness as a struggler for communism cannot be reconciled with the existence of God. And like Bakunin he saw religion essentially as an instrument in the hands of the exploiters. In consequence, Lenin's attack on religion is self-consciously militant, his theomachy shrill, his blasphemy bitter. And, for Lenin, theomachy—the struggle against God—is the other side of the historical coin of class struggle, what he called the "struggle against socio-economic bondage."

Georgi Valentinovich Plekhanov, although self-taught in philosophy and the social sciences, was an erudite and versatile writer, Lenin's chief mentor in theoretical philosophy, and for many years the intellectual "senior statesman" of the Russian Marxist movement. He was born in 1856, in Tambov province, and studied first at a military *gymnasium* in Voronezh and then at a military college in St. Petersburg. Upon graduation he resigned his commission (as Bakunin had done a generation before) and entered the St. Petersburg School of Mining Engineering.

From 1875 to 1883 Plekhanov was a Populist (*Narodnik*) and quite close to Bakunin's anarchist position. He rejected political institutions, stressed the role of the peasants' village commune (*obshchina*), and glorified such peasant rebels as the eighteenth-century Emelyan Pugachyov. Plekhanov lived illegally (without an internal passport) in 1879 and 1880, when he fled to Switzerland.

He became a Marxist in 1883, the year of Marx's death, but, ironically, he derived his first "great respect" for Marx from reading some of the more "Marxist" writings of Bakunin. He knew and corresponded with Engels (1889–95) and was closely associated with Lenin in Geneva from the mid-1890's until 1903, when he refused to join either the Menshevik or Bolshevik faction of the party, and became increasingly critical of the Bolsheviks. (Plekhanov rejected the program of Lenin's *What Is to Be Done?* as "peasant insurrectionism.") He condemned the 1905 revolution as premature and he supported the Allies against the Central Powers in 1914, repudiating Lenin's view that the First World War was an "imperialist brawl" in which Marxists should take no sides.

Plekhanov returned to Petrograd shortly after the February revolution of 1917. Kerenski offered him a post in the provisional government but Plekhanov declined it, although he supported Kerenski against the Bolsheviks and was bluntly critical of the policies of Lenin and Trotsky. He died in Finland in May, 1918.

In our discussion of Lunacharski we saw that Plekhanov was essentially an eighteenth-century *philosophe*, reminiscent to some extent of Diderot, although less subtle and elegant as a thinker and writer, both in his philosophical materialism and his attitude toward religion. This attitude was neatly characterized by Berdyaev, who wrote in 1932: "His struggle against religion is intellectual, scholarly in character. He still thinks that religious beliefs will die out as a result of the growth of enlightenment among the masses." Berdyaev went on to note that this "good-natured and mocking" attitude, typical of the *Aufklärer*, neglects what the Leninists consider central, namely, "the class character of religion and the necessity of a class-religious struggle against it."[9]

Plekhanov was willing to admit that "religious beliefs impair the development of the self-consciousness of the working class and serve as an opium which lulls the proletariat to sleep."[10] However, despite such references to class consciousness it is clear that Plekhanov's view, like that of Engels, admits the possibility of the "abolition of religion independently of the social revolution, simply in terms of the progress of science."[11]

Plekhanov's characteristic position is that the anti-religionist should not "abuse or upbraid, but enlighten."[12] Because religion is essentially "bad" (i.e., primitive and defective) science, it can be eliminated most effectively by mass education in the "good" sciences, accompanied by mass indoctrination in the philosophical principles of what Plekhanov christened "dialectical materialism." (Neither Marx nor Engels had used the term, although Engels had used the parallel term 'historical materialism'.)

Plekhanov maintained that all religions, not just primitive ones, are animistic. The product of attempts to purge religion of animism is not religion at all but morality in a broad sense. This applies to Buddhism, which remains animistic, even though it is in a sense "atheistic." And it applies to Tolstoy, whose attempt to purge his religious teaching of animistic and supernatural elements was ultimately a failure. Plekhanov insists that

[9] N. A. Berdyaev, Generalnaya liniya sovetskoi filosofii i voinstvuyushchi ateizm [The General Line of Soviet Philosophy and Militant Atheism] (Paris, 1932), p. 21; English trans. in The End of Our Time: Together with an Essay on the General Line of Soviet Philosophy, trans. Donald Attwater (New York, 1933), pp. 246 f.

[10] G. V. Plekhanov, "Svyashchennik G. Gapon" [The Priest G. Gapon] (1905), in Sochineniya (Moscow-Leningrad, 1926), 13:198.

[11] Lobkowicz, "Marx's Attitude toward Religion," p. 327.

[12] Plekhanov, "Svyashchennik G. Gapon," p. 199.

morality predates religion and has no need whatever of religious sanction.[13]

Although Plekhanov distinguished between religious ideas or conceptions (*predstavleniya*), i.e., myths; religious attitudes or moods (*nastroyeniya*), i.e., feelings; and religious actions (*deistviya*), i.e., cult or worship, he tended to stress the first of these to the virtual exclusion of the others.[14] This is nicely brought out in his response to the questionnaire of the French journal, *Mercure de France* (1907), that includes the statement: "As for religious feeling or conviction, it will disappear with the dissolution of the religious idea."[15] Presumably, religious cult or worship will follow suit.

In Plekhanov's view the "remedy" for the persistence of religious belief in Russia, whether before or after the "social revolution," is atheistic education and indoctrination, public lectures on popular science (with an anti-religious slant), and huge printings of cheap editions of the works of Lucretius, Rabelais, Voltaire, Diderot—and, of course, Feuerbach, Marx, and Engels—in good, readable Russian translations.

In some places Plekhanov—reversing the order of Hegel's historical and dialectical sequence—suggests that religion may be transitional not to knowledge or science but to art. And perhaps he would see art as transitional to science. He sometimes implies that the main function of art, on the one hand, is to popularize scientific truths, and on the other hand to propagate "correct" moral values and social attitudes.

[13] "O tak nazyvayemykh religioznykh iskaniyakh v Rossii" [On the So-called Religious Searchings in Russia], in *Sochineniya*, 17:232–35, 237.

[14] *Sochineniya*, 17:197, 229 f.

[15] The French text reads as follows: "Quant au sentiment religieux, il disparaîtra avec la dissolution de l'idée religieuse" (66:619).

Taking a cue from Schiller's *Letters on the Aesthetic Education of Mankind*, Plekhanov suggested that churches should eventually be replaced by theaters. When this happens, he declared, religion, which is in fact a product of the human imagination but masquerades as truth about the real world, will give way to art, which is in fact truth about the real world that modestly presents itself as a mere product of the human imagination.

Such a claim, of course, presupposes a particular theory of art, namely, the "mimetic" or representational theory, according to which art "reflects" the objective reality of nature, man, and society. Plekhanov was, in fact, one of the founders of the Soviet doctrine of "socialist realism." The edge of his distinction is turned against the rival view of art as a free "creation" or "expression." It is not the poet or painter, Plekhanov argues, but the priest or theologian who creates freely; that is, in abstraction from social and historical reality, uncontrolled by the "facts of the case." Man, he liked to say (with Feuerbach), "creates God in his own image and likeness."[16] In this view theology, more truly than poetry, is mythopoeic.

Plekhanov's final comment on religion is accompanied by an urbane lift of the Marxist eyebrow at the thought that "educated and intelligent people," such as Tolstoy, could find intellectual or even emotional satisfaction "in the world view of old peasant women."[17]

---

[16] In *Sochineniya*, 27:230. This creation may take fairly elaborate "sociomorphic" forms (to borrow a term from Berdyaev). Thus in deism, God's power "is limited on all sides by the laws of nature. Deism is heavenly parliamentarianism" (that is, the god of the deists is not an absolute but a limited monarch). *Ibid.*, p. 231 (italics removed).

[17] In L. I. Akselrod, *Etyudy i vospominaniya* [Studies and Reminiscences] (Leningrad, 1925), p. 39.

III

The difference in style of anti-religious utterance between Plekhanov and Lenin is striking. Plekhanov, who considered religion an intellectual error, is relatively restrained and scholarly; Lenin, who considered religion a social and moral outrage, is furiously indignant and desperately abusive. Lenin, quite understandably impatient with Plekhanov's moderate and subdued approach, insisted, with obvious reference to Plekhanov, that the fight against religion must not be limited to "abstract intellectual preaching" but must invariably be related to the "concrete practical class movement," that is, to class struggle.

Because, according to Lenin, "the oppression of mankind by religion is merely a product and reflection of economic oppression within society," the proletariat must be "enlightened" not by "books or preaching" but by "its own struggle against the dark forces of capitalism." Lenin is not satisfied with "enlightenment brochures," and he explicitly warns against "an abstract, idealistic formulation of the religious question 'by reason' apart from class struggle."[18]

Lenin's own neo-Marxist theory of religion involves two basic assumptions, one concerning the *origin*, the other the *function* of religious beliefs, attitudes, and institutions. The first assumption is that religion is generated by human insecurity and fear of unanticipated and uncontrollable socio-economic change, due in the last analysis to the fluctuations of the "free" market. The second assumption is that religion invariably functions as a tool of the exploiting classes, as an "opium" (Lenin's blunter expression was "spiritual booze") that dulls and lulls the exploited masses into resigned acceptance of their bondage, forestalling

[18] V. I. Lenin, "Sotsializm i religiya" [Socialism and Religion] (1905), in *Sochineniya*, 5th ed. (Moscow, 1960), 12:146; English trans. in Lenin, *Collected Works* (Moscow, 1962), 10:86.

revolt here and now with the promise of an other-worldly reward for virtuous obedience to the secular rulers.

In addition to this primary socio-political or public function, Lenin of course recognized a secondary, psychological or personal function of religion: that of restoring the individual believer's shattered sense of security, quieting his animal fears—all at the level of myth or "false consciousness." But Lenin and his followers have been much less interested in such "subjective" factors than in the "objective" factors at work in history and society. They have paid little attention to the psychology of belief or the phenomenology of the religious consciousness. There is nothing whatsoever in Russian Marxist literature to compare with William James' *Varieties of Religious Experience*.

Lenin saw religion as a form of "stupefaction" (*odureniye*) or "stultification" (*oduracheniye*) of the working class, echoing terms that were used by both Bakunin and Tolstoy (see chapter 1). The suffering and hardship caused by oppressive socio-economic conditions, Lenin insists, are a thousand times worse than the suffering and hardship caused by such natural catastrophes as floods and earthquakes.

The idea of God, he wrote, echoing Bakunin (and Feuerbach), derives from the "crass submissiveness of man" in the face both of external nature and class oppression. Fear of the blind forces of the capitalist socio-economic system is "*the* taproot of modern religion."

The impotence of the exploited classes in their struggle with the exploiters generates faith in a better life beyond the grave just as inevitably as the impotence of the savage in the struggle with nature generates faith in gods, devils, miracles, etc. Religion teaches the man who labors and is in want his whole life long to have forbearance and patience in this earthly life, consoled by the hope of a heavenly reward. Religion teaches those who live by the labor of others to give charity in this earthly life, offering them a very cheap

141

justification for their whole exploitative existence, selling them tickets to heavenly bliss at a reasonable price. Religion is the opium of the people. Religion is a kind of spiritual booze or schnapps (sivukha) in which the slaves of capital drown their human image, their demands for a life in some degree worthy of man.[19]

Lenin in 1905 was quite confident that religious belief was a "delirium" that was "rapidly being thrown into the rubbish-barrel by the very course of economic development," that is, by the "logic" of Marxist history.[20] The contemporary class-conscious worker, he added, "scornfully repudiates religious prejudices, leaving heaven to the priests and to sanctimonious members of the bourgeoisie."[21] But the language of such passages, which suggests an automatic elimination or discarding of religion, is not typical of Lenin.

Lenin's characteristic position is that revolutionaries should neither stand aside, letting religion automatically "wither away," nor limit themselves to anti-religious propaganda. "Waiting" is not enough, and "preaching" is not enough. To do away with religion one must take active steps to cut its socio-economic root, freeing the worker "from belief in a life beyond the grave by rallying him to a genuine struggle for a better earthly life," for the "creation of heaven on earth."[22]

Lenin's reference to the "creation of heaven on earth" suggests that he was committed to a Promethean historical project, even though, unlike Plekhanov, he made little if any explicit reference to Prometheus or Prometheanism. Plekhanov, as early as 1892, was quite ready to declare that

[19] "Sotsializm i religiya," pp. 142 f.; Collected Works, 10:83 f. (italics removed).

[20] "Sotsializm i religiya," p. 146; Collected Works, 10:87.

[21] "Sotsializm i religiya," p. 143; Collected Works, 10:84 (italics removed).

[22] Ibid., pp. 143, 146, and pp. 84, 87.

contemporary socialism is carrying out just such a task as the Greeks ascribed to Prometheus. It is giving men the means with which they will put an end to their dependence on blind, elemental forces and will subject those forces to the dominion of reason, thus attaining an unprecedented development.[23]

The Prometheanism of Plekhanov and Lenin differed from the Prometheanism of the "God-builders" Gorky and Lunacharski mainly in rhetoric and emphasis. The rhetoric of Gorky and Lunacharski was exalted and romantic; that of Plekhanov and Lenin was generally down-to-earth and businesslike. The "God-builders" emphasized the "religious" dimension of the Promethean task; Plekhanov and Lenin insisted on purging their Marxist Prometheanism of every remnant of religious language and symbolism, however "secularized" or "socialized." They insisted that religion of every kind should, and eventually would, wither away with the approach to socialism. As we shall see in chapter 6, the current Soviet variety of Prometheanism stands between the two versions, but measurably closer to the tradition of Plekhanov and Lenin than to that of Gorky and Lunacharski.

Lenin's early attitude toward religious freedom and the relation of church and state was a seemingly "liberal" one. As early as 1902, in a draft program of the Russian Social-Democratic (Marxist) Party, prepared jointly by Plekhanov and Lenin (among others), we find two relevant planks: "(4) unlimited freedom of conscience, speech, press, assembly, [the right to] strike and [to form or join] unions," and "(10) separation of church from state and of school from church."[24]

[23] Plekhanov, "O zadachakh sotsialistov v borbe s golodom v Rossii" [On the Tasks of the Socialists in the Struggle against Famine in Russia] (1892), in Sochineniya (Moscow-Petrograd, 1923), 3:399–400.

[24] "Proyekt programmy Rossiiskoi sotsial-demokraticheskoi rabochei partii" [Draft Program of the Russian Social-Democratic Workers' Party], in Lenin,

In December, 1905, Lenin asserted that the Russian revolutionary movement must work for the complete separation of church and state. And he added:

Everyone should be completely free to profess any religion at all or not to accept any religion, i.e., to be an atheist, which is what every socialist will usually be. Distinctions between citizens as to their rights, made on the basis of religious beliefs, are wholly inadmissible. Even the mention of a citizen's religious faith in official documents should be unconditionally abolished. There should be no allotment of funds to a state church . . . or to . . . religious societies; these should become wholly free unions of like-minded citizens (grazhdane-yedinomyshlenniki), independent of [i.e., not supported by] the political authority.[25]

Lenin went on to attack the Russian Orthodox "state church" and the "medieval, inquisitorial laws" of the tsars, which "persecuted people for their [non–Russian Orthodox] faith or lack of [Russian Orthodox] faith."[26]

In the draft of a speech prepared for delivery before the second Duma (Russian parliament) in 1907, Lenin insisted that his party stood for "complete freedom of conscience and [had] full respect for all sincere conviction in matters of faith, so long as this conviction is not impressed upon others by violence or deception."[27] Just how sincere Lenin may have been in his defense of freedom of conscience is difficult to say.[28] In

Sochineniya, 5th ed. (Moscow, 1959), 6:206; English trans. in Lenin, Collected Works (Moscow, 1961), 6:30.

[25] "Sotsializm i religiya," pp. 143 f.; Collected Works, 10:84.

[26] "Sotsializm i religiya," p. 144; Collected Works, 10:84.

[27] "Proyekt rechi po agrarnomu voprosu vo vtoroi gosudarstvennoi dume" [Draft of a Speech on the Farm Question in the Second State Duma] (1907), in Lenin, Sochineniya, 5th ed. (Moscow, 1961), 15:157; English trans. in Collected Works (Moscow, 1962), 12:296.

[28] According to a recent commentator, "Lenin's motives were those of a political strategist rather than humanitarian. 'Freedom of conscience,' far from being considered an end in itself . . . , is treated by him as a . . .

any case he made it very clear that there could be no toleration of religious commitment in the ranks of the party:

We demand that religion should be a private matter so far as the state is concerned, but under no circumstances can we consider religion a private matter so far as our own Party is concerned.[29]

Lenin warned that the party "must not be indifferent to"—that is, must actively combat—"lack of class-consciousness (*bessoznatelnost*), ignorance, and obscurantism in the form of religious beliefs" among party members. He added that one of the main reasons for organizing a Marxist party in Russia was to "carry on the struggle against all religious bamboozling or stultification (*oduracheniye*) of the workers. For us, therefore, the ideological struggle is not a private affair but the affair of the whole Party, of the whole proletariat."[30]

Lenin's assumptions about the source and function of religion as well as his program for separation of church and state and for the general struggle against religious commitment were translated into legislation and public policy during the early years of the Bolshevik regime. We shall look more closely at that process and its results in chapter 6.

---

tactical weapon," intended, among other things, to exploit religious dissent for political purposes. See Bohdan R. Bociurkiw, "Lenin and Religion," in *Lenin: The Man, the Theorist, the Leader*, ed. Leonard Schapiro and Peter Reddaway (London: Pall Mall; New York: Praeger, 1967) pp. 112–13.

[29] "Sotsializm i religiya," p. 143; *Collected Works*, 10:84.

[30] "Sotsializm i religiya," p. 145; *Collected Works*, 10:86. We may note the systematic ambiguity of the Leninist comma, as used in the last phrase: ". . . the affair of the whole Party, of the whole proletariat" (in Russian: . . . *obshchepartiinoye, obshcheproletarskoye delo*). The *prima facie* and innocent sense of the comma is "as well as"; the much stronger sense, clearly intended by Lenin, is "that is to say." Lenin and contemporary Marxist-Leninists regularly insinuate such strong equations (e.g., "of the Party and the proletariat" or "the people") by the seemingly harmless use of conjunctive commas.

6

RELIGION AND ANTI-RELIGION
IN THE SOVIET UNION

I

On January 21, 1918, Lenin's government published a law
defining the rôle and status of religion in the new Soviet society.
The law was originally titled "On Freedom of Conscience, and
on Ecclesiastical and Religious Societies," and apparently had
been drafted without Lenin's explicit approval. When it reached
his desk he made two significant changes: he changed the title
to "The Separation of Church from State and of School from
Church" and he deleted the statement in the body of the
law that "religion is a private affair," substituting "The church
is separated from the state."[1] Broadly speaking, this law was
modeled on an earlier French law (1905) on separation of
church and state but it went beyond the French law in several
respects, attempting to establish not only a secular but also (with
the help of additional legislation in 1929) an atheistic society.

First, there was the expropriation of church property. Not
only land and buildings but icons, altars, and even crosses be-

[1] Both texts have been published in *Kommunisticheskaya partiya i sovetskoye pravitelstvo o religii i tserkvi* [The Communist Party and the Soviet
Government on Religion and the Church] (Moscow, 1959), pp. 39–43.

146

came "public property" that could be used only by being leased from the Soviet government. This provision differed in only two minor respects from its French model. (1) The French government in 1905 stipulated that church buildings and objects of worship could be "leased" without charge by local congregations; the Soviet law specified a rental charge. (2) The French law was not enforced, and later was softened, mainly because of resistance from the church hierarchy, whereas the Soviet law was firmly enforced from the 1920's and was less rigidly enforced only during and after the Second World War.

Second, there was the prohibition (in 1929) of religious instruction. Children under eighteen years of age were permitted to receive religious instruction only in groups of no more than three, and only in private homes. (The training of priests was permitted until the late 1920's, and resumed in the 1940's.)

Finally, there was the stipulation, as in the French law—and even in the French "Declaration of the Rights of Man and the Citizen" of 1789 (Article 10)—that there should be no interference with citizens' religious views "provided their expression does not disturb the public order." In the interpretation and application of this proviso the Soviet government, as we shall see, went far beyond the French law.

The Soviet constitution of 1936, promulgated by Stalin and to this day (1968) the law of the land, underscores the differential treatment accorded believers and non-believers. The former have the "right to worship" and are free to believe in "any god whatever," while atheists have the "right and every opportunity" to unite for formulating and promulgating anti-religious propaganda.

There is no equality here, even on paper. Believers have the right to believe and to worship but they are denied the right to instruct others and to attempt to persuade others to share their belief. In contrast, non-believers have not only the right to disbelieve but also the right, opportunity, and systematic encouragement of the party and the state to attempt to persuade others to share their atheism. In addition, the massive Soviet apparatus of formal education and of formal and informal indoctrination is used, of course, entirely on the side of the non-believers.

Soviet spokesmen repeatedly asserted during the 1920's and 1930's that the struggle against religion was to be carried on soley through persuasion, without resort to force. Nevertheless, open coercion against political subversion and "counterrevolution" often touched religiously sensitive points, as in the arrest, imprisonment, exile, and (in many cases) execution of large numbers of priests and monks, as well as in the expropriation of church and monastery lands and the nationalization of ecclesiastical farms, workshops, and printing presses.[2] Other measures, less public and sometimes deliberately concealed from foreign visitors, were equally coercive. Disciplinary action, including expulsion, was applied against Young Pioneers and Komsomol (Young Communist League) members who attended church. Non-party young people could be disciplined at school, and even expelled from school, for such an offense.

The law of 1918 specified that religious worship must not interfere with either the work or the leisure of Soviet citizens—but the "leisure-time" activities of Soviet citizens were permitted, even deliberately organized, to interfere with religious worship. Noisy dances were scheduled at Christmastime and Eastertime in halls next to those churches that remained open.

[2] In 1918 alone, Soviet authorities arrested "scores of [Russian Orthodox] bishops and hundreds of priests" (William C. Fletcher, *A Study in Survival: The Church in Russia, 1927–1943* [London, 1965], p. 15).

A good deal of "spontaneous" vandalism also was directed against the churches. During and following the first five-year plan (1928–32) there was, in the words of one commentator, a wave of "vandalism unprecedented in the history of modern times: between 1929 and 1934 hundreds, if not thousands, of churches, including many historic monuments, were destroyed."[3]

In order to lease a church building each congregation had to elect a responsible *dvadtsatka* or "committee of twenty." If the membership of this committee dropped below twenty (as a result of death, arrest, retirement, or change of residence of its members), the congregation was allowed only two weeks in which to find replacements. If its attempts at recruitment failed, the congregation could be dissolved and the church closed. Government agents, moreover, could infiltrate a *dvadtsatka*, gain a "legal" majority, and vote the dissolution of the congregation.[4] Church buildings thus "freed" were either destroyed outright or converted into warehouses, workshops, garages, club houses, dance halls, or lecture halls. An example of the conversion of a church into a lecture hall: the high-domed "Polish [Roman Catholic] church" in Kiev is now a planetarium where astronomy lecturers purvey anti-religious propaganda.

During the 1920's and 1930's Komsomol leaders attacked the "backward" and "unsanitary" practice of kissing icons and protested the waste of Soviet natural resources in the cutting of Christmas trees. School children were urged to sign petitions complaining that church bells kept them awake or interfered

[3] Nikita Struve, *Les Chrétiens en U.R.S.S.*, 2d ed. (Paris, 1964), pp. 44 f. Struve appends a list of more than one hundred Orthodox bishops who were killed or who disappeared between 1918 and 1938.

[4] See Fletcher, *A Study in Survival*, pp. 60 f. The 1929 law included a formal provision for so-called "religious groups" having fewer than 20 members. However there is no clear evidence that such "groups" were actually permitted to function.

149

with their studies, and should be removed. In the villages youngsters were told to "borrow" their parents' Bibles, which were then piled in a corner of the schoolroom and, at an appropriate moment, consigned to the flames. Anti-religious parades were staged during the principal religious holidays, featuring floats on which drunken "priests" cavorted with scantily clad "prostitutes."

All this was reflected in a 1923 resolution passed by the Twelfth Congress of the Soviet Communist Party to the effect that anti-religionists should not "offend the feelings of believers, since this would only lead to an increase in their religious fanaticism. The deliberately coarse methods frequently applied at the center [i.e., in Moscow, the administrative center] and locally, the mocking of objects of faith and worship, . . . do not expedite but hamper the emancipation of the working masses from religious prejudices."[5]

Organizational measures were grandiosely conceived. In 1928 Yemelyan Yaroslavski (né Gubelmann), who since 1925 had headed the Union of the Militant Godless (Soyuz Voinstvuyushchikh Bezbozhnikov), announced an anti-religious five-year plan. The union was to attain a membership of 17 million, the newspaper Bezbozhnik was to reach a circulation of 250,000, and the "scholarly" journal Antireligioznik was to reach a circulation of 60,000. The figures achieved in 1932, though sub-

[5] Kommunisticheskaya partiya Sovetskovo Soyuza v rezolyutsiakh i resheniyakh s'ezdov, konferentsi i plenumov Ts K [The Communist Party of the Soviet Union in Resolutions and Decisions of Congresses, Conferences, and Plenary Sessions of the C. C. (Central Committee)], 7th ed., pt. 1 (Moscow, 1953), p. 744; partly quoted in Bolshaya Sovetskaya Entsiklopediya [Large Soviet Encyclopedia], 2d ed. (Moscow, 1955), 36:339. The encyclopedia quotation ends with the word 'fanaticism,' thus omitting all reference to the "coarse methods" of anti-religious agitation criticized in the party resolution.

stantially lower than the goals, were impressive: more than 5.5 million members of the union and circulations of 199,500 for *Bezbozhnik* and 31,900 for *Antireligioznik*.[6] By 1938, according to some reports, *Antireligioznik* had reached a circulation of 60,000.

Not all of the 5.5 million members of the Union of Militant Godless were actively militant. It is doubtful that more than two million fell into that category; the remainder were more or less passive and perfunctory "dues paying" members. In contrast, Soviet printing presses were feverishly active. During just three months in 1930, 13 million anti-religious pamphlets were published. There was an endless stream of lectures, exhibits, and posters on Darwinism, geology, astronomy, and physiology, all with an atheistic orientation.

Yaroslavski confidently predicted that by the completion of the second five-year plan (i.e., by 1937) no churches would remain open in the Soviet Union. A. V. Lunacharski, whose "religion of God-building" we examined in chapter 4 and who served as People's Commissar for Education until 1929, was more realistic. In the early 1930's he confessed, presumably with a sigh, that "religion is like a nail: the harder you hit it, the deeper it goes in."

An official census that was completed in 1937, the year after the "achievement of socialism" had been officially announced, reportedly turned up the awkward fact that 57 percent of Soviet citizens—about 80 million people—were ready to declare themselves "religious believers," in a socio-economic climate where such a declaration could do them no personal or professional good and might do them considerable harm. This was

[6] See Struve, *Les Chrétiens en U.R.S.S.*, p. 46.

151

the first time Stalin's census-takers had asked such a question. For obvious reasons it was also the last! (And the census of 1937 remained unpublished.)

Because one might be tempted to conclude that the overwhelming majority of the 80 million "believing" Soviet citizens were peasants, it is worth reporting that—in Yaroslavski's own estimate—only two-thirds of them came from the adult rural population and as many as one-third were from the adult urban population.

The great turning point for religion in the Soviet Union came in the period 1941–44. Within a few months after Hitler's attack on the Soviet Union Stalin's government had dissolved the Union of the Militant Godless and suspended both *Bezbozhnik* and *Antireligioznik*; by 1944 it had reinstated the Moscow patriarch, whose office since 1925 had been held only by a *locum tenens*, reopened several theological seminaries, and begun printing theological literature on government printing presses (there were no others). These startling concessions— put into effect between 1941 and 1944—were primarily a reward to the Russian Orthodox faithful for their support of the Soviet war effort. Significant but much less dramatic concessions were made to other religious groups.

Early in 1964, at the height of Khrushchev's anti-religious campaign of 1959–64, Ilyichev, the leading Soviet ideologist of the day, declared publicly that one of Stalin's major crimes had been an inexcusable softness toward religion! But Stalin, as it happened, attached a few political strings to his concessions, especially in the immediate postwar period. After 1949 high officials of the Russian Orthodox church regularly endorsed Soviet-sponsored "peace campaigns," and the venerable Patriarch

Alexi, in connection with his seventy-fifth, eighty-fifth, and ninetieth birthdays (November, 1952 and 1962, and January, 1968), was decorated with the Order of the Red Banner of Labor in recognition of his "great patriotic activity in the struggle for peace."

Alexi and the Russian Orthodox synod earned their Stalinist and post-Stalinist accolades. In 1952 the synod formally condemned "imperialist aggression," including "germ warfare," in Korea. In the same year representatives of all the religious groups that were recognized by the Soviet authorities gathered at Zagorsk, where each representative not only called for support of the Soviet "struggle for peace" (e.g., in Korea) but also heaped personal praise upon Stalin. In 1956 the synod— although somewhat vaguely and ambiguously—supported the Soviets' suppression of the Hungarian revolution. And in November of 1962 Patriarch Alexi sent a message to all "heads of state, religious leaders, and Christians" deploring the action of the United States government in the Cuban missile crisis.[7]

Alexi's "Christmas message for 1965" echoed *Pravda* editorials on Vietnam. "Strangers from distant lands," he wrote, "are waging a bloody war in South Vietnam. Their air force is carrying out combat missions on a widening scale over the territory of the sovereign state of the Democratic Republic of [North] Vietnam. . . . The waterspout of war which rages over ancient Vietnam spares neither women nor children nor the old." The "foreigners," Alexi added, the "bearers of death and destruction in Vietnam," are guilty of "cruelty and lawlessness." He called for an end of bombing in North Vietnam, an end of military action in the south, and the subsequent withdrawal of all

[7] For additional examples of political statements by the Russian Orthodox hierarchy, see Struve, *Les Chrétiens en U.R.S.S.*, pp. 78–80.

foreign troops—in a word, he endorsed the "peace program" of Hanoi and the Vietcong.[8]

All this would seem to be a far cry from the "absolute separation of church and state" that Lenin and the other early Russian Marxists had advocated.

II

Although the blunt and primitive phase of Soviet anti-religious *agitation* came to an abrupt end during the Second World War, many of the forms of anti-religious *propaganda* that were initiated in the 1920's continue in force today, with only minor shifts of emphasis.

Two of the most common forms of anti-religious propaganda, aimed primarily at the young, deal not with religion directly but with the social and moral manifestations and consequences of religious practices and institutions.

In its *negative* form such propaganda undertakes to generate revulsion toward religious beliefs and practices by means of "chambers of horrors," as a part of the anti-religious exhibits and museums that often are set up in unused churches (the most famous of these "chambers" is in the former Kazan Cathedral in Leningrad). The gory details of the tortures practiced by the Spanish and Portuguese inquisitions, priests blessing the armies of "imperialism," and Prussian cannons marked *Gott mit uns* are prominently displayed to huge audiences. In 1960 alone, 500,000 persons visited the Leningrad museum, an average of almost 1,400 per day.[9] What is more important, there

---

[8] *Zhurnal Moskovskoi Patriarkhii* [Journal of the Moscow Patriarchate], no. 2 (1966), p. 2. Writing in 1965, Fletcher declared: ". . . it would appear that today the Church has lost most of the concessions won for it by [Patriarch] Sergii [beginning in 1927], while the services it must render to the State have, if anything, increased" (*Study in Survival*, p. 120).

[9] See Struve, *Les Chrétiens en U.R.S.S.*, p. 245.

154

were 6,083 group visits, mostly by school children, and each group (the average was almost seventeen groups per day) received a guided tour and a detailed anti-religious commentary by a member of the museum's large staff.

An early statement carries such negative propaganda to a truly Leninist pitch of abusiveness. Its author, a man named Loginov, declared that the bourgeoisie, the "most cynical, blood-thirsty, and unconscionable of all beasts—that two-legged beast of prey— . . . has acknowledged the god of Palestinian savages as its own class god, a divine protector of the exploitative order and of military plundering, a god of the rich, a god of ignorance, oppression, and immorality."[10] The anti-religious propaganda of the 1960's is generally less abusive than this (although there have been vehement exceptions, notably in the propaganda directed at Judaism), but the message is still essentially the same.

Similarly with *positive* anti-religious propaganda, which continues to project an "affirmative image" of the atheist by appealing to the "great atheists" of Russian history, such men as Chernyshevski, Herzen, and Pavlov. And here we find a curious mixture of historical truth, half-truth, and untruth. Chernyshevski, a priest's son, was in fact a theist-turned-atheist, and Herzen was a theist-turned-agnostic, but the academician Pavlov—like the pioneering genius of Soviet rocket technology, Konstantin Tsiolkovski—remained a devout Russian Orthodox believer to the end of his days.

III

Khrushchev's anti-religious campaign of 1959–64 (some aspects of which still continue, at a slightly moderated pace) repeated

[10] A. Loginov, "Religiya i nravstvennost" [Religion and Morality], in *Kommunizm i religiya* [Communism and Religion] (Moscow, 1922), p. 199.

many features of the campaigns of 1928–32 and 1937–40, although without recourse to the primitive forms of anti-religious agitation that marked these earlier periods. A Western commentator refers to the 1959–64 campaign as "one of the longest and most implacable [anti-religious campaigns] that the [Russian Orthodox] Church had been subject to."[11] Of course, the religious "minority groups" in the Soviet Union: the schismatic Old Believers, the Roman Catholics, Protestants, Jews, Mohammedans, Buddhists, and others—were also included in the new assault.

Khrushchev's methods tended to follow the letter of the Soviet law (including some new laws that were introduced for the purpose) but often they violated the spirit of its earlier "non-application." Thus the agreements for leasing church buildings, originally made with German occupying forces and quietly honored for the next twenty years, were abruptly nullified and the churches were closed (this happened mainly in the Ukraine and Belorussia). Priests were accused—twenty years later—of having collaborated with the Germans during the Second World War; they were dismissed, and in many cases jailed. Other priests were charged with trying to "lure" children to church services, and in a few cases with attempting to build new churches.

As in the 1920's and 1930's, the device of the "undersize" *dvadtsatka* ("committee of twenty") was widely employed. Priests were forbidden to serve more than one parish, and the "surplus" parishes were closed. Income taxes of up to 83 percent were levied on the salaries of the clergy although the maximum was 13 percent for other Soviet citizens, no matter how high their income. The sale of church candles was attacked as "specu-

[11] Struve, *Les Chrétiens en U.R.S.S.*, p. 259.

lation," thus jeopardizing as much as 75 percent of the revenue of the Russian Orthodox church. Church buildings were condemned on all of the familiar pretexts, and on some new ones as well. If they were close to school buildings they were said to influence the impressionable minds of the youngsters adversely (many Soviet schools are located near churches because they are housed on former parochial-school premises). In the cities it was said that the larger churches attracted excessive crowds, which interfered with traffic.

A new article (no. 227) of the penal code of 1962 forbids the "organization" or "direction" of religious groups whose activities may "injure the health" of citizens or cause "non-fulfillment by citizens of their social or civic obligations," and outlaws the enrollment of minors in such groups, under the maximum penalty of five years' imprisonment. The law has been applied against baptismal rites, the kissing of icons, and other religious practices. Since 1962 priests and ministers have been permitted to baptize children only upon a written application from both parents, supported by a certificate from their place of work or residence. The authorities who issue these certificates are expected to have done everything possible in dissuading the "misguided" parents.

I shall omit further details,[12] noting only some statistical results of the new campaign. Russian Orthodox sources claim that 10,000 Orthodox churches have been closed since 1959. Official Soviet sources confirm this statement, giving the number of churches that functioned before 1959 as 20,000 to 22,000 and the number of functioning churches early in 1962 as 11,500. (According to other Soviet sources, the drop was from more than 15,000 to 7,500.) The number of priests is said to have

[12] See *ibid.*, ch. 12 (pp. 255–95).

157

fallen from 30,000 before 1959 to 14,500 early in 1962.[13]

It is unlikely that religious commitment has been reduced in corresponding ratios; indeed, there are many indications that, despite the new persecutions, this number has actually increased. One bit of evidence is that, in the face of the new obstacles to baptism, the rate of baptisms has gone up in many areas. In 1964 a Soviet anti-religionist complained that nearly half of the babies then being born in the Soviet Union were being baptized, citing this statistic as evidence of the need for a renewed surge of anti-religious propaganda directed at younger people. Western commentators estimate the range from 100 percent in some rural areas to 30 and 50 percent in the cities, the nation-wide average being close to 70 percent—in any case well above half.[14]

In 1961 Patriarch Alexi reported that the total number of Russian Orthodox faithful was between 20 and 30 million, and there seems little reason to question this figure. All other religious groups in the Soviet Union, taken together, might add another 15 to 20 million. Thus one can say with confidence that there are some "tens of millions" of the churched in the Soviet Union. However, even if the figure were as high as 50 million (which seems unlikely), it would amount to only a little more than one-fifth of the total Soviet population of 240 million.

It is clearly and significantly the case, moreover, that in Soviet society the churched fall into the lowest socio-economic and educational strata. Almost all of the churched are peasants, unskilled workers, minor service workers, and minor clerical

[13] N. Yudin, *Pravda o peterburgskikh svyatynyakh* [The Truth about the Holy Places of Petersburg] (Leningrad, 1962), p. 8; cited in Struve, *Les Chrétiens en U.R.S.S.*, pp. 263, 276. The number of churches functioning in 1925 was officially put at 39,000 and at 30,000 in 1930, (cf. *Izvestiya*, February 19, 1930; cited in Fletcher, *Study in Survival*, p. 45).

[14] Cf. Struve, *Les Chrétiens en U.R.S.S.*, p. 155.

employes. Only a tiny fraction of the churched have more than a secondary-school education; some, especially in the country-side, have only primary education. (In part, of course, this is due to official obstruction of higher education for religiously-committed Soviet citizens.)

In terms of age and sex distribution, the middle-aged and older outnumber the young, and women outnumber men. The fact that there are today almost three women for every two men in the adult (over age twenty-one) Soviet population is a result of the great purges of the 1930's, when several million men but almost no women were killed, and of Soviet military and civilian losses during the Second World War, when male fatalities greatly outnumbered female fatalities.[15]

It seems evident that the overwhelming majority (probably close to 90 percent) of Soviet citizens with higher education are unchurched. A small but important group among this over-whelming majority (as I shall indicate presently) is "religious," although it stands "outside the walls of the church." Some-what larger groups have accepted one or another of the current

[15] According to the Soviet census of 1959, the percentage of females of all ages in the total population exceeded 55 percent; of the adult popula-tion, at least 60 percent were women. Struve estimates the percentage of women among the churched at 70 to 80 percent. Many of them are old, but, as Struve points out, it is very difficult to estimate the age of Russian peasant women. All those over thirty look "about the same age" and all those over forty look "old" (Les Chrétiens en U.R.S.S., p. 161). Ilyichev officially admitted that 30 percent of Soviet churchgoers are under forty, and this figure is supported by my own recent observations and those of other Western visitors (my six visits to the Soviet Union span the period 1956–68). One extra-religious reason for these relative disproportions is that women and older people do not generally hold responsible positions in Soviet society that church affiliation would place in jeopardy. In the Soviet Union most non-peasant women over fifty-five and most men over sixty are retired on pensions, and many individuals deliberately defer church attend-ance until they are retired and no longer have careers to worry about.

pseudo-religions (see below). The remainder, probably a decisive majority of the 90 percent, are atheists or agnostics. The reductionist critique of religion as "bad science" à la Plekhanov and the eighteenth-century *philosophes* seems to have been accepted by most Soviet university graduates under the age of about forty-five.

I have already distinguished between intellectual, social, and spiritual or strictly religious aspects or dimensions of religion (pp. 7–8). The historically rooted de-emphasis of social concern, which I mentioned earlier, has quite understandably been encouraged and intensified by the Soviet authorities. Since 1929 church groups have been forbidden by law to engage in any kind of charitable, educational, or recreational activity.[16] Until that time some groups, chiefly Protestant and schismatic, had engaged in a modicum of charitable and social activity.

Thus in their attacks on religion Soviet anti-religionists can safely ignore the *social* dimension; and as a matter of practice they have largely ignored the *spiritual* dimension as well. They have, of course, attacked religious morality, insisting, for example, that the "obsolete" Christian virtues of forbearance, humility, and brotherly love must be replaced by the "up to date" socialist virtues of devotion to the collective, pride in one's Soviet motherland, and implacable hatred toward her enemies. The late Professor Gagarin, a leading exponent of "scientific atheism" (a discipline that is pursued in special academic departments in Soviet universities), declared in 1951 that religious morality "impels people to parasitism" and undermines faith in the "omnipotence of Communist labor."[17]

[16] Cf. Fletcher, *Study in Survival*, p. 46.

[17] A. P. Gagarin, *O klassovom kharaktere religioznoi morali* [On the Class Character of Religious Morality] (Moscow, 1951), p. 25.

Soviet commentators implicitly admit that their critique of religiously based morality has been theoretically slight. They explicitly admit that their critique reduces to only three points: (1) exhibiting the alleged "class" character of religious morality, (2) showing the incompatibility of religious principles with the principles of communist morality, and (3) criticizing the specific moral teachings of the Bible, the Koran, and other holy books.[18]

The chief target of Soviet anti-religious propaganda has always been the *intellectual* content of religion—not theology in the strict sense but mere (mostly incidental) assertions or denials of scientific facts or theories, for example, Darwinism. The Soviet anti-religious dialogue proceeds at the level of the Scopes "monkey trial" of 1925, but it is not a genuine dialogue inasmuch as spokesmen for religious groups have no public opportunity to answer their atheist critics. The latter are free to pursue their "Plekhanovite" reduction of religion to doctrine, to a kind of science—but "bad science," pseudo-science.[19]

The success of this religiously irrelevant critique is evidenced by the fact that most Soviet citizens with higher education who were born after the revolution are convinced that religion is "unscientific," if not downright superstitious, and is not to be taken seriously by anyone with intellectual pretensions. This also is true of many Soviet citizens who remain unconvinced by, or are indifferent to, the official Marxist-Leninist philosophy and ideology. Generally speaking, the negative aspects of this

[18] Cf. G. L. Andreyev *et al.*, "Nauchny ateizm za 50 let" [Fifty Years of Scientific Atheism], *Voprosy Filosofii*, no. 12 (1967), p. 43.

[19] Since 1959 the "Plekhanovite" propaganda has been massive. In 1962, 355 anti-religious books and pamphlets, with a total printing of 5.4 million copies, were published. This was double the total for 1930, the previous record year. See Struve, *Les Chrétiens en U.R.S.S.*, p. 244.

ideology—its destructive critique of religion and capitalism—
find much wider acceptance than its positive assertions about
man and the world.

IV

From the viewpoint of Marxism-Leninism, the continuing
although relative vitality of religion in the Soviet Union presents a serious doctrinal problem. The failure of religion to
"wither away" at the present advanced stage of transition from
socialism to communism—more than half a century after the
October revolution—is now "explained" as a result of new
insecurity and fear that has been generated in the Soviet popu-
lace by the threat of thermonuclear war. Because, in the official
account, such a war would be launched only by "capitalist"
governments, the persistence of religion in Soviet society is
explained as a result—indirect rather than direct—of the evils
of the capitalist socio-economic system! (Lip service is still paid
to explanation in terms of "capitalist survivals," but in the
fifty-first year of the revolution this has diminished plausibility.)

To be sure, religion is still expected to wither away completely with the "approach to full communism," but the party
program of 1961 avoids assigning a date for its final disappear-
ance. Indeed, a spokesman for Russian Orthodoxy declared
publicly a few years ago that, with the attainment of full communism, religion would truly begin to flower! No official Soviet
spokesman has gone this far, but various straws in the recent
ideological wind (since ca. 1965) suggest that the Soviet authorities are reconciled to the indefinite persistence of religion under
socialism, and perhaps even under full communism.

Thus book reviews in Nauka i Religiya [Science and Reli-
gion]—the successor to Antireligioznik, which began publication in 1959—have been noting that various books should be of

interest not only to atheists, anti-religious propagandists, historians, anthropologists, and the like but also "to the believing reader" (*veruyushchi chitatel*). This same phrase is used in the cover blurb of K. K. Platonov's new book, *Psikhologiya religii* [The Psychology of Religion], published in Moscow in 1967. The blurb concludes: "This book will be read with profit not only by propagandists and people interested in the problems of scientific atheism and psychology, but also by believing readers."

Even more indicative of this attitude is the fact that the official account of anti-religious activities in the half-century of Soviet rule does not once use the phrase "withering away of religion" or "withering away of the church." It notes, instead, that recent studies "permit us to understand better the present status of the Orthodox church, and to predict the *paths of its possible development*."[20]

From a non-Marxist viewpoint, on the other hand, the relative *weakness* of religious feeling and commitment in the Soviet Union, especially among the better-educated, presents a problem (although the level of religious commitment in the Soviet Union is probably about as high as that in France or Sweden, where there have been no organized anti-religious campaigns). In addition to the success of the reductionist anti-religious critique there is another, less obvious fact. Soviet society as a whole—state, party, school, farm, and factory—has for many years been engaged in eroding the privacy of Soviet citizens, and individuals in the Soviet Union have had only limited success in resisting this erosion although many have made strenuous efforts to do so.

If, as William James and Alfred North Whitehead have sug-

[20] Andreyev *et al.*, "Nauchny ateizm za 50 let," p. 41 (italics added).

gested, religion is "what a man does with his solitude," the waning of religious feeling in the Soviet Union is quite understandable. Solitude in the James-Whitehead sense presupposes at least a modicum of privacy, and lack of privacy would adversely affect both traditional and non-traditional forms of religious commitment (see below).

A mandatory, official collectivism also has tended to displace traditional religions in the Soviet Union. To some degree this collectivism has become a kind of secular pseudo-religion, providing a new kind of "opium" for the "power elite" of Soviet society. I distinguish two species of this secular pseudo-religion. (1) Orthodoxly atheistic Marxism-Leninism, accepted by only a tiny and dwindling group, attracts perhaps 1 or 2 percent of the total population, and this group is confined almost entirely to the *aktiv* of the party and the Komsomol.[21] (2) A scientific-technological Prometheanism reaches a much larger, perhaps slowly expanding group, a group drawn mainly from the Soviet scientific and technical elite. Despite Lenin's repudiation of the "religion of God-building," pseudo-religious Prometheanism in various forms has continued to flourish throughout the Soviet period.

One form of Prometheanism has been closely tied to theomachy. "We declare war on the old gods," exclaimed an early anti-religionist; "long live the new man—maker and creator—who not only equals but far surpasses them."[22] Another and more durable form has been more explicitly technological in its means and more flamboyantly utopian in its ends. An early Russian Marxist, whose works were republished under Soviet

---

[21] Of course, 1 percent of the total Soviet population is 2.4 million people and 2 percent is 4.8 million people.

[22] M. A. Reisner, *Nuzhna li vera v boga?* [Is Belief in God Necessary?] (Moscow, 1923), p. 128.

auspices in the 1920's, declared that we have no conception of the extent of man's eventual power over nature. In the remote future *homo faber* "will take possession of the universe and extend his species into distant cosmic regions." Eventually, a perfected science and technology will stretch man's life expectancy to the point where human beings will achieve physical immortality! "We, who are now struggling for a [Marxist] social ideal, are struggling, in the final analysis, . . . for individual immortality."[23]

Five years later N. A. Rozhkov, a Marxist economic historian, added that within a few centuries scientists would work out mathematical formulas expressing the configuration of electrons in any given human organism, thus preventing diseases of every kind. Medicine, he wrote, "will be able to prolong life almost indefinitely. . . . It is conceivable that even the dream of eternal youth will be realized." Rozhkov made an even more startling statement: "We mortals may hope to *awaken*"—even a photograph of a dead person or a fragment of a letter he had written will provide sufficient clues for reconstructing the unique individual formula of his electrons.

Men who lived many centuries ago will be resurrected in the chemical laboratory. And, of course, they [in turn] will resurrect those whom they knew and loved. The task of immortality (*zadacha bessmertiya*) will finally be carried out. We must try to be worthy of future resurrection.[24]

The project of achieving physical immortality, and even of raising the dead, had also been put forward by N. F. Fyodorov (1828–1903) at the end of the nineteenth century. But his

[23] "NN" (anonymous author), *O proletarskoi etike* [On Proletarian Ethics] (St. Petersburg, 1906), p. 39.
[24] N. A. Rozhkov, *Osnovy nauchnoi filosofii* [Fundamentals of Scientific Philosophy] (St. Petersburg, 1911), pp. 131, 132 (italics added).

"projective" philosophy of the "common task"—a collective effort to overcome "non-brotherhood" and "dis-relatedness"— was moral and religious both in motivation and terminology.[25] Rozhkov and the Marxists secularized and vulgarized it.

Short of the "Prometheanism unbounded" of physical immortality (a highly ambiguous concept because anyone, however old, who claims to be physically immortal may die the moment after he makes the claim), there is the project for dramatically increasing the average life expectancy. In a poem of the 1920's the Soviet poet Vladimir Mayakovski spoke of the "eternally youthful" centenarian who would "*do sta rasti bez starosti*" ["live to a hundred without old age"]. And Howard Fast asserted publicly in 1951, when he was still a Stalinist, that the progress of Soviet science was bringing an "indefinite extension" of man's life-span within the realm of possibility. When pressed by a questioner whether this implied the eventual realization of physical immortality, he smiled and replied that this was not impossible but that the prospects then in view were only for a life expectancy of "some tens of thousands of years"![26]

If such claims seem too fanciful to be taken seriously we may look to more moderate Soviet statements. A Moscow medical journal declared in 1961: "To live a long time, even if living forever is denied us, that is a goal that all people are striving for."[27] A "long time" had been defined by academician

[25] Fyodorov's article, "The Question of Brotherhood . . . ," slightly abridged, has been translated into English by Ashleigh E. Moorehouse and myself in *Russian Philosophy*, ed. James M. Edie, James P. Scanlan, Mary-Barbara Zeldin, and George L. Kline (Chicago; Quadrangle Books, 1965), 3:16–54.

[26] For a survey of Russian and Soviet work on the "prolongation of life" and speculations on physical immortality, see Peter Wiles, "Physical Immortality," *Survey*, nos. 56 and 57 (1965).

[27] *Sovetskoye Zdravokhraneniye* (December, 1961), p. 88; quoted in Wiles, "Physical Immortality," no. 56, p. 125.

V. A. Obruchev as "150 to 200 years on the average." Obruchev added that Soviet citizens "rightly demand" from Soviet science and technology such a prolongation of life, together with the elimination of infectious diseases, overcoming "old age and fatigue," the restoration of life "in cases of untimely accidental death," and so on.[28]

Another Soviet scientist, Vladimir Keler, asserted in 1966 that the average life expectancy would increase gradually until it reaches one hundred by the year 2000; then, in the twenty-first century, "if wanted, life will be continued for any period, even centuries." He added, in a kind of inverse Fyodorovian vein, that "hereditary memory will be revived . . . people will awake to their past and remember what their forefathers lived through and saw hundreds, thousands, and perhaps millions of years back."[29]

Soviet scientists, however, have said nothing in recent years about Rozhkov's Fyodorovian project of the physical resurrection of the dead.

Climate control, interplanetary colonization, prolongation of life to the point of eventual physical immortality—these stand as the Promethean goals that have crowded traditional religion, as well as such non-Marxist philosophies as existentialism, out of the minds of the majority of better-educated Soviet citizens. In this sense every Soviet space success is indeed, as

[28] Obruchev's statement was highlighted by being placed—in a footnote —near the end of the standard ideological textbook Osnovy Marksizma-Leninizma ([Moscow, 1959], pp. 752–53). Several million copies of this book are in print in many different languages. In the official English translation, Obruchev's statement is made part of the text. See Fundamentals of Marxism-Leninism (Moscow, 1963), p. 716.

[29] "Yesterday, Today, Tomorrow," Soviet Life (September, 1966), p. 13 (italics added).

the official propagandists never tire of repeating, a blow against religion. One doubts, however, that what Thomas Blakeley has called the "cosmonautological proof" of atheism is taken very seriously: Soviet cosmonauts who have traveled through outer space have not seen God; therefore God does not exist. Nevertheless, the anti-religious thrust of the space program is still emphasized, as in a 1965 painting, prominently displayed in the Kazan Cathedral, of a priest gazing meditatively at Soviet newspaper headlines which announce a manned space flight. The title of the painting is "Razdumye"—"Second Thoughts."

The displacement of traditional religious values by the values of a scientific-technological Prometheanism was succinctly symbolized by a slogan which I saw in 1957 scrawled—presumably by a young atheist—across the wall of a church near Kiev, the city sacred to the memory of St. Vladimir, who brought Christianity to Russia. It read: "Flight to the Moon, 1973."

V

The genuinely religious surrogate for traditional religion is limited to a small but apparently growing group of young Soviet intellectuals—mainly poets, writers, and artists—and an increasing number of university students. Their position may be defined, tentatively, as a "philosophical" and non-ecclesiastical theism, in some cases quite close to pantheism.[30] These young intellectuals and students are inspired by three giants of twentieth-century Russian literature: Marina Tsvetayeva, who died in 1941; Boris Pasternak, who died in 1960; and Anna Akhmatova, who died in 1966.

[30] I have surveyed the religious aspects of recent Soviet poetry and fiction, published and "underground," in a paper entitled "Religious Themes in Soviet Literature," which will be published in Aspects of Religion in the Soviet Union, ed. Richard H. Marshall, Jr.

Tsvetayeva and Akhmatova were devoutly Orthodox through-out their lives, and this is reflected in their poetry, especially in that of Tsvetayeva. Both women were under a cloud for many years and remained virtually unpublished in the Soviet Union from the 1920's until 1961. In that year small volumes of their selected poetry (and Pasternak's) were published, although carefully purged of all religious poems. In 1965 large volumes of the works of all three writers appeared, including a few of the explicitly religious poems, though with many omissions (especially in the case of Tsvetayeva). Just how widely known the suppressed poems are is very difficult to determine, but many of the younger poets know and are influenced by them. When Akhmatova died, her funeral, like Pasternak's six years earlier, was conducted in the Orthodox rite. Unlike Pasternak's, however, it was public, announced in the Soviet press, and immediately reported abroad.

Pasternak, although he came to Christianity relatively late and expressed an explicitly religious viewpoint in his work only during the last decade of his life, is perhaps the greatest single force promoting sympathy for and interest in religion among the young poets and intellectuals in the Soviet Union. This does not mean that they wholeheartedly accept his "re-invented" Christianity (although some of them do); nevertheless, they are impressed by the seriouness and the freshness of his religious feeling and by his view of Christianity as a religion that fuses "sacrificial love" and "creative freedom."

Pasternak's later religious poems exhibit a depth of feeling and vividness of imagery that may be unique in modern literature since the poetry of Rilke. Dr. Zhivago, like most of Pasternak's religious poetry, has not yet been published in the Soviet Union and is available only in the "cultural underground." Neverthe-less, the publication in 1965 of two or three of his later religious

169

poems in the large one-volume edition of his poetry, with a long and appreciative introductory essay by Andrei Sinyavski (at that time not yet publicly known to be "Abram Tertz"), is an event of great potential significance.[31]

It has become evident in the past few years that Sinyavski, who is now serving a seven-year term at hard labor, Solzhenitsyn, who has been bitterly attacked for permitting his last two major works, Cancer Ward and In the First Circle, to be published abroad, and Tarsis, who emigrated to the West in 1966, are all believing Christians. However, religious themes in their works are almost entirely limited to their unpublished writings or to works published only outside the Soviet Union (which, of course, are circulated among the literati in Moscow, Leningrad, and Kiev).

Stalin's daughter, Svetlana Alliluyeva, though of questionable stature as a writer, is important as fresh testimony to the presence of religious convictions in the upper reaches of the Soviet social and intellectual hierarchy. Her religious beliefs, however undefined and elusive, seem to be perfectly sincere.

In recent works of the younger "Leningrad poets"—especially Joseph Brodsky—religious motifs are clear and strong. As yet, however, their poetry is virtually unpublished in the Soviet Union although it is quite widely known in Soviet literary and intellectual circles, both in manuscript form and through the Russian-language editions published abroad.

Brodsky and his friends know and value the religious thought of Shestov and Berdyaev, and even of the lonely nineteenth-century thinker Chaadayev. Tarsis has said that he knew and treasured the religious philosophy of Rozanov, Berdyaev, and

---

[31] Soviet authorities have announced that Dr. Zhivago is to be published in 1969 as the final volume (vol. 7 or 8) of the complete works of Pasternak.

Solovyov while he was still in Moscow (he received émigré editions of their works from correspondents abroad). He adds that many of his younger associates in Moscow had similar intellectual interests.

All of this suggests that some of the religious thinkers examined in the earlier chapters of the present study—especially Rozanov, Berdyaev, and Shestov, and perhaps Leontyev and Tolstoy—may be in the process of being "rediscovered" in a significant way by a minority among the youngest generation of Soviet intellectuals. Such a rediscovery could scarcely fail to set in motion a widening and deepening erosion of the rival Soviet pseudo-religions, doctrinaire Marxism-Leninism and scientific-technological Prometheanism.

171

INDEX

INDEX

174